Medicare Made Easy: Benefits for American Retirees

Copyright Page

TITLE: Medicare Made Easy: Benefits for American Retirees

1ST Edition

Table of Contents

Medicare Made Easy: Benefits for American Retirees

By Roberto Miguel Rodriguez

Chapter 1: Introduction to Medicare

Understanding Medicare

Medicare is a vital healthcare program that provides benefits to American retirees and their families. This subchapter aims to provide a comprehensive understanding of Medicare, its various components, and the wide range of benefits it offers to retirees. Whether you are approaching retirement or have already retired, it is crucial to have a clear understanding of Medicare to make informed decisions regarding your healthcare needs.

Medicare Made Easy: Benefits for American Retirees is a valuable resource that simplifies the complexities of Medicare, making it easier for retirees and their families to navigate the system. This subchapter will delve into the different aspects of Medicare, ensuring that you have a solid grasp of its benefits and coverage options.

The subchapter will begin by explaining the different parts of Medicare, including Part A (hospital insurance) and Part B (medical insurance). It will explore the eligibility criteria, enrollment process, and the costs associated with each part. Additionally, it will highlight the importance of Medicare prescription drug coverage (Part D) and how it can help retirees manage their medication expenses effectively.

Furthermore, this subchapter will shed light on the advantages of Medicare Advantage plans for retirees. It will discuss the additional benefits and services offered by these plans, such as dental, vision, and hearing coverage, as well as the importance of choosing the right plan based on individual needs.

Retirees will also gain insights into Medicare supplemental insurance options, also known as Medigap, which can help cover out-of-pocket costs that Original Medicare does not cover. It will address the various

Medigap plans available and how they can provide financial security and peace of mind.

Moreover, this subchapter will explore Medicare coverage for preventive services, chronic disease management, mental health services, home healthcare services, skilled nursing facility care, and hospice care. It will emphasize the importance of preventive care and managing chronic conditions to ensure a healthy and fulfilling retirement.

Lastly, it will touch upon Medicare coverage for durable medical equipment, such as wheelchairs, walkers, and oxygen equipment, which play a crucial role in maintaining independence and quality of life for retirees.

By the end of this subchapter, retirees and their families will have a comprehensive understanding of Medicare and its various components. Armed with this knowledge, they will be able to make informed decisions about their healthcare needs, ensuring they receive the maximum benefits and coverage available to them through Medicare.

History and Evolution of Medicare

Introduction:

Medicare is a vital program that provides healthcare coverage to millions of American retirees and their families. Understanding the history and evolution of Medicare is crucial in order to appreciate the benefits it offers today. This subchapter explores the journey of Medicare from its inception to its current form, highlighting the significant milestones and changes that have shaped this essential program.

Origins of Medicare:

The idea of a national healthcare program for older Americans was first introduced in the early 20th century. However, it was not until 1965 that

Medicare was enacted into law under President Lyndon B. Johnson. The program was a response to the growing healthcare needs of the elderly population and aimed to provide them with affordable and accessible healthcare.

Medicare Expansion:

Initially, Medicare consisted of two parts: Part A, which covered hospital insurance, and Part B, which covered medical insurance. Over the years, the program has seen several expansions to meet the evolving healthcare needs of retirees. In 2003, Medicare Part D was introduced, offering prescription drug coverage. This addition brought immense relief to retirees who were struggling with the rising costs of medications.

Advancements in Medicare:

In recent years, Medicare has introduced various advancements to enhance coverage options for retirees. Medicare Advantage plans, also known as Part C, provide an alternative to Original Medicare and offer additional benefits such as vision, dental, and hearing coverage. This has given retirees more flexibility in choosing the healthcare services that best suit their needs.

Supplemental Insurance Options:

Medicare supplemental insurance, also known as Medigap, has become increasingly popular among retirees. These plans help fill the gaps in coverage left by Original Medicare, including deductibles, copayments, and coinsurance. Medigap plans offer peace of mind, ensuring that retirees are not burdened with unexpected out-of-pocket expenses.

Expanded Coverage:

In recognition of the importance of preventive care, Medicare has expanded its coverage to include various preventive services. These services include screenings, vaccines, and annual wellness visits, all aimed at detecting potential health issues early and promoting overall well-being.

Focus on Chronic Disease Management and Mental Health Services:

Medicare has also recognized the significance of chronic disease management and mental health services for retirees. Through specialized programs, Medicare aims to provide comprehensive care and support to those dealing with chronic conditions and mental health issues.

Home Healthcare, Skilled Nursing Facilities, and Hospice Care:

Medicare coverage extends beyond hospital stays and doctor visits. It includes home healthcare services, allowing retirees to receive necessary care in the comfort of their own homes. Additionally, Medicare covers skilled nursing facility care and hospice care, ensuring that retirees have access to the appropriate care settings during times of illness or end-of-life.

Accessibility to Durable Medical Equipment:

Another invaluable aspect of Medicare is its coverage for durable medical equipment. This includes devices such as wheelchairs, walkers, and oxygen equipment, which are essential for many retirees in maintaining their mobility and independence.

Conclusion:

The history and evolution of Medicare have transformed it into a comprehensive healthcare program that is vital for American retirees and their families. From its humble beginnings, Medicare has expanded its coverage options and benefits to meet the growing and diverse needs of retirees. Understanding the journey of Medicare allows retirees to fully appreciate the invaluable support it offers in ensuring their health and well-being throughout their retirement years.

Eligibility Requirements for Medicare

Chapter Summary: In this subchapter, we will explore the eligibility requirements for Medicare, the federal health insurance program designed to provide coverage for American retirees and their families. Understanding these requirements is crucial in order to determine if you qualify for Medicare and to navigate the enrollment process effectively.

Medicare is available to individuals who meet specific criteria, including age, disability status, and certain medical conditions. The eligibility requirements for each part of Medicare may vary, so it is essential to understand the distinctions. Let's delve into the various eligibility criteria for Medicare and its different components.

Age-Based Eligibility: Most retirees become eligible for Medicare at age 65. Individuals who have worked and paid Medicare taxes for at least ten years are automatically eligible for Medicare Part A, which covers hospital insurance. Part B, which covers medical insurance, is also available at this age, but it requires enrollment and a monthly premium.

Disability-Based Eligibility: People under 65 can also qualify for Medicare if they have received Social Security Disability Insurance (SSDI) benefits for at least 24 months or have end-stage renal disease (ESRD) or amyotrophic lateral sclerosis (ALS).

Specific Medical Conditions: Medicare also covers individuals of any age with specific medical conditions, such as ESRD and ALS. These individuals can qualify for Medicare, regardless of their age, without the usual waiting period.

Enrollment Periods: It is crucial to understand the enrollment periods for Medicare to avoid any gaps in coverage or late enrollment penalties.

The Initial Enrollment Period (IEP) begins three months before the month of your 65th birthday and ends three months after. The General Enrollment Period (GEP) occurs annually from January 1 to March 31. Additionally, there are Special Enrollment Periods (SEP) for those who qualify due to employment, among other circumstances.

In this subchapter, we have explored the eligibility requirements for Medicare. Whether you are approaching age 65, have a disability, or suffer from specific medical conditions, it is important to understand the criteria for each aspect of Medicare coverage. By familiarizing yourself with these requirements, you can ensure that you and your loved ones receive the benefits you deserve.

Chapter 2: Medicare Basics

Medicare Parts A, B, C, and D

One of the most significant challenges that retirees and their families face is understanding the complexities of Medicare. With so many different parts and coverage options available, it can be overwhelming to navigate through the maze of information. In this chapter, we will break down Medicare Parts A, B, C, and D to help you better understand what each part entails and how it can benefit you as an American retiree.

Medicare Part A covers hospital stays, skilled nursing facility care, hospice care, and some home health care services. This part is often referred to as hospital insurance and is automatically provided to most people when they turn 65. Part A helps cover the cost of inpatient hospital stays, including room and board, as well as various skilled nursing facility services that are necessary for your recovery. Additionally, it provides coverage for hospice care for individuals with terminal illnesses and limited coverage for home healthcare services.

Medicare Part B is known as medical insurance and covers outpatient care, doctor's visits, preventive services, and medical supplies. This part requires a monthly premium and is optional, but highly recommended. Part B helps cover the cost of doctor visits, lab tests, outpatient surgeries, preventive services like flu shots and screenings, and durable medical equipment such as wheelchairs and walkers.

Medicare Part C, also known as Medicare Advantage plans, is offered by private insurance companies approved by Medicare. These plans provide all the benefits of Part A and Part B, with additional coverage options such as prescription drugs, dental, and vision services. Medicare Advantage plans often include prescription drug coverage, which brings us to Medicare Part D.

Medicare Part D is dedicated solely to prescription drug coverage. This part helps pay for prescription medications and is also offered by private insurance companies. It is important to note that Part D is optional, but highly recommended, as it can significantly lower your out-of-pocket costs for prescription drugs.

Understanding the different parts of Medicare is crucial for retirees and their families. Depending on your healthcare needs and preferences, you may choose to enroll in Original Medicare (Parts A and B) and add additional coverage through Medicare Advantage plans, Medicare supplemental insurance, or Part D prescription drug plans. By familiarizing yourself with these options, you can make informed decisions about your healthcare coverage and ensure that you receive the benefits you deserve as an American retiree.

Medicare Enrollment Process

The Medicare enrollment process is a vital step for retirees and their families to access the benefits that Medicare offers. Understanding how to enroll in Medicare can help you navigate the system and ensure you are receiving the coverage you need. In this subchapter, we will guide you through the Medicare enrollment process, providing you with the necessary information to make informed decisions about your healthcare coverage.

To begin, it is important to note that there are specific enrollment periods for Medicare. The initial enrollment period is when most people become eligible for Medicare, which is typically around their 65th birthday. This seven-month period includes the three months before your birthday, the month of your birthday, and the three months following your birthday. It is crucial to enroll during this period to avoid any late enrollment penalties.

There are several ways to enroll in Medicare. One option is to visit the Social Security Administration website and complete an online application. Alternatively, you can call the Social Security Administration or visit your local office to apply in person. If you are already receiving Social Security benefits, you will be automatically enrolled in Medicare Parts A and B.

It is important to understand the different parts of Medicare and the coverage they provide. Medicare Part A covers hospital stays, skilled nursing facility care, home healthcare services, and hospice care. Medicare Part B covers doctor visits, preventive services, durable medical equipment, and mental health services. To receive prescription drug coverage, you can enroll in Medicare Part D, which is provided by private insurance companies. Additionally, there are Medicare Advantage plans (Part C) and Medicare supplemental insurance options (Medigap) that can provide additional coverage and help with out-of-pocket costs.

Once you have enrolled in Medicare, it is essential to review your coverage annually during the open enrollment period. This allows you to make any necessary changes to your plan to ensure it meets your healthcare needs for the upcoming year.

In conclusion, the Medicare enrollment process is a crucial step for retirees and their families to access the benefits and coverage they need. By understanding the enrollment periods and the different parts of Medicare, you can make informed decisions about your healthcare coverage. Don't forget to review your coverage annually during the open enrollment period to ensure it continues to meet your needs.

Medicare Coverage Periods

Understanding the different coverage periods under Medicare is crucial for retirees and their families to make informed decisions about their healthcare needs. This subchapter aims to provide a comprehensive overview of the various coverage periods available under Medicare, ensuring that American retirees can maximize their benefits.

Medicare coverage is divided into several periods, each serving a specific purpose. The first period to consider is the Initial Enrollment Period (IEP). This is the seven-month window that begins three months before an individual turns 65 and extends three months after. It is during this period that retirees can enroll in Medicare Part A and/or Part B.

Another important coverage period is the Annual Enrollment Period (AEP), which occurs from October 15th to December 7th each year. During this time, retirees can make changes to their Medicare Advantage plans or Medicare prescription drug coverage. It is essential to review and compare plans to ensure they align with individual healthcare needs and budget.

The Medicare Advantage Open Enrollment Period (MA OEP) takes place from January 1st to March 31st annually. This period allows individuals already enrolled in a Medicare Advantage plan to switch to another plan or return to Original Medicare. It is a great opportunity to reassess healthcare needs and explore different coverage options.

Additionally, the Medicare General Enrollment Period (GEP) runs from January 1st to March 31st each year. This period is for individuals who missed their Initial Enrollment Period and did not qualify for a Special Enrollment Period. During the GEP, individuals can enroll in Medicare Part A and/or Part B, but coverage will not start until July 1st.

Understanding these coverage periods is crucial for retirees and their families to take full advantage of Medicare benefits. It is recommended to consult with a Medicare specialist or use online resources to navigate the complexities of the different periods and make informed decisions.

In the following chapters, we will delve deeper into each coverage period, discussing the specifics, eligibility requirements, and potential pitfalls to avoid. By understanding the Medicare coverage periods, retirees and their families can ensure they have the right coverage for preventive services, chronic disease management, mental health services, home healthcare services, skilled nursing facility care, hospice care, and durable medical equipment.

Medicare Made Easy: Benefits for American Retirees is your guide to navigating the intricacies of Medicare coverage periods and making informed decisions that will safeguard the health and well-being of retirees and their families.

Medicare Costs and Premiums

One of the essential aspects to consider when planning for retirement is understanding Medicare costs and premiums. As retirees and their families, it is crucial to be well-informed about these financial aspects to ensure a smooth transition into Medicare coverage. In this subchapter, we will explore the various costs and premiums associated with Medicare and how they may impact your healthcare expenses.

Medicare is a government-funded program that provides health insurance to individuals aged 65 and older, as well as those younger with certain disabilities. However, while Medicare covers a significant portion of healthcare expenses, it is important to be aware that there are still costs involved.

Medicare Part A, which primarily covers hospital stays, usually does not require a premium if you or your spouse paid Medicare taxes while working. However, there are deductibles and coinsurance amounts that need to be considered. For example, in 2022, the Medicare Part A deductible is $1,548 per benefit period.

Medicare Part B, which covers doctor visits and outpatient services, does require a monthly premium. The standard premium for 2022 is $170.10, but it may vary based on your income. Additionally, there is an annual deductible of $233 that needs to be met before Medicare starts paying its share.

Medicare Part D is the prescription drug coverage portion of Medicare. It is provided by private insurance companies approved by Medicare. The costs for Part D plans can vary significantly, including premiums, deductibles, copayments, and coinsurance. It is essential to carefully review and compare different plans to find the one that best suits your prescription drug needs.

Medicare Advantage plans, also known as Part C, are an alternative to Original Medicare. These plans are offered by private insurance companies and provide all the benefits of Part A and Part B, along with additional benefits such as prescription drug coverage. The costs for Medicare Advantage plans can vary, including premiums, deductibles, and copayments.

To further protect yourself from out-of-pocket expenses, you may consider Medicare supplemental insurance, also known as Medigap. These plans are sold by private insurance companies and help pay for costs not covered by Original Medicare, such as deductibles and coinsurance.

Understanding Medicare costs and premiums is crucial for retirees and their families to plan for their healthcare expenses effectively. By being aware of these financial aspects, you can make informed decisions and ensure that you have adequate coverage while managing your budget during retirement.

Chapter 3: Medicare Prescription Drug Coverage

Overview of Medicare Prescription Drug Coverage (Part D)

Medicare Prescription Drug Coverage, also known as Part D, is an essential component of Medicare that provides coverage for prescription drugs. This subchapter aims to provide an overview of Part D, explaining its benefits and how it works, addressing the needs of retirees and their families.

Medicare Part D is a voluntary program available to individuals who have Medicare Part A and/or Part B. It helps cover the costs of prescription drugs, including both brand-name and generic medications. This coverage is provided through private insurance companies approved by Medicare.

One of the most significant advantages of Part D is that it offers protection against high prescription drug costs. It ensures that retirees have access to the medications they need at an affordable price. Part D plans have a list of covered drugs, known as a formulary, which includes most commonly prescribed medications. However, it is crucial to review the formulary to ensure that specific medications are covered.

To enroll in a Part D plan, retirees can choose between standalone Prescription Drug Plans (PDPs) or Medicare Advantage Prescription Drug (MA-PD) plans. PDPs work alongside Original Medicare, while MA-PD plans combine prescription drug coverage with Medicare Advantage benefits, providing a comprehensive healthcare package.

When selecting a Part D plan, retirees should consider factors such as monthly premiums, deductibles, copayments, and the pharmacies included in the plan's network. It is essential to review these details carefully to find a plan that best meets individual healthcare needs and budget.

Part D coverage includes different phases, including the initial deductible phase, the initial coverage phase, the coverage gap (or "donut hole") phase, and the catastrophic coverage phase. The specifics of each phase can vary depending on the plan chosen, but they are designed to ensure that retirees receive appropriate coverage throughout the year.

Additionally, Part D plans offer opportunities for cost savings, such as generic drug substitution, medication therapy management programs, and mail-order pharmacy options. These options can help retirees save money on their prescription medications while ensuring they receive appropriate care.

In conclusion, Medicare Prescription Drug Coverage (Part D) plays a vital role in providing affordable access to prescription medications for retirees. It is essential for retirees and their families to understand the benefits and options available to them under Part D to make informed decisions about their healthcare. By exploring the various Part D plans and considering personal healthcare needs and budget, retirees can find the most suitable coverage for their prescription drug needs.

How to Choose a Medicare Prescription Drug Plan

Choosing a Medicare prescription drug plan can be a daunting task, especially with the numerous options available. However, with some careful consideration and understanding of your needs, you can select the best plan that suits your requirements and provides adequate coverage for your prescription medications. In this subchapter, we will guide you through the essential steps to help you make an informed decision.

1. Assess Your Medication Needs: Begin by creating a list of all the prescription drugs you currently take, including dosages and frequencies.

This will help you determine which plans cover your medications and at what cost.

2. Compare Plans: Medicare offers a tool called the Plan Finder on its official website, which allows you to compare different prescription drug plans available in your area. Consider factors such as monthly premiums, annual deductibles, copayments, and the pharmacy network.

3. Formulary Analysis: Each prescription drug plan has a formulary, which is a list of drugs covered by the plan. Ensure that the plan you choose covers all or most of your medications. Be aware of any restrictions or limitations imposed on certain drugs.

4. Consider Total Costs: In addition to premiums, consider other costs associated with the plan, such as deductibles and copayments. Some plans offer coverage in the coverage gap or "donut hole." Evaluate your potential out-of-pocket expenses to find the most cost-effective plan.

5. Review Pharmacy Networks: Verify that your preferred pharmacy or pharmacies are included in the plan's network. Some plans may require you to use specific pharmacies or offer additional benefits for using preferred pharmacies.

6. Seek Assistance: If you find the process overwhelming, seek help from trained professionals or Medicare counselors who can provide personalized guidance and answer your specific questions.

7. Annual Reevaluation: Remember that your prescription drug needs may change over time. It is vital to review your plan annually during the Medicare Open Enrollment Period (October 15 to December 7) to ensure it still meets your needs.

Choosing the right Medicare prescription drug plan can save you money and ensure you have access to the medications you need. By following these steps and taking the time to evaluate your options carefully, you can confidently select a plan that fits your needs and provides peace of mind for both retirees and their families. Remember, proper medication coverage is essential for maintaining your health and well-being during retirement.

Coverage Gap (Donut Hole) and Catastrophic Coverage

As retirees and their families navigate the complex world of Medicare, it's important to understand the intricacies of coverage gaps and catastrophic coverage. In this subchapter, we will delve into the details of the Coverage Gap, also known as the Donut Hole, and the protection offered by Catastrophic Coverage.

Medicare prescription drug coverage is a vital component of your healthcare plan, but it's crucial to be aware of the Coverage Gap. The Coverage Gap refers to a temporary limit on what your Medicare drug plan will cover for prescription medications. Once you and your plan have spent a certain amount on covered drugs, you enter the Coverage Gap. During this phase, you are responsible for a higher percentage of the costs.

However, it's essential to note that the Coverage Gap is gradually closing. Medicare has been implementing changes to reduce the burden on beneficiaries. For instance, if you enter the Coverage Gap, you qualify for a discount on brand-name prescription drugs, reducing your out-of-pocket expenses.

Catastrophic Coverage provides further protection once you have reached the out-of-pocket threshold for prescription drug costs. Once you reach this threshold, you only pay a small coinsurance amount or a copayment for covered drugs for the remainder of the year. Catastrophic Coverage ensures that you are not financially overwhelmed by high drug costs, providing peace of mind during challenging times.

To ensure you make the most of your Medicare coverage, it's important to explore additional options such as Medicare Advantage plans and Medicare supplemental insurance. These plans can help fill the gaps in your coverage and provide additional benefits, such as dental, vision, and hearing care.

Additionally, Medicare offers coverage for a wide range of services, including preventive care, chronic disease management, mental health services, home healthcare, skilled nursing facility care, hospice care, and durable medical equipment. Understanding the scope of these services can help you access the care you need and make informed decisions about your healthcare.

In conclusion, being aware of the Coverage Gap and Catastrophic Coverage is vital for retirees and their families to navigate the Medicare landscape successfully. By exploring additional options like Medicare Advantage plans and supplemental insurance, you can enhance your coverage and protect yourself from unexpected healthcare costs. Moreover, understanding the breadth of services covered by Medicare ensures you receive the necessary care for preventive, chronic, mental health, and home healthcare needs. With Medicare Made Easy, you can confidently make informed choices for your healthcare journey.

Chapter 4: Medicare Advantage Plans for Retirees

Introduction to Medicare Advantage Plans (Part C)

Medicare Made Easy: Benefits for American Retirees

Welcome to the subchapter on Introduction to Medicare Advantage Plans (Part C) from our book, "Medicare Made Easy: Benefits for American Retirees." This section is specifically tailored to retirees and their families, helping you navigate the complexities of Medicare Advantage Plans.

Medicare Advantage Plans, also known as Part C, are an alternative to Original Medicare (Parts A and B) offered by private insurance companies approved by Medicare. These plans provide comprehensive coverage that combines hospital insurance (Part A), medical insurance (Part B), and often prescription drug coverage (Part D) in one convenient package.

One of the key advantages of Medicare Advantage Plans is the additional benefits they offer beyond what Original Medicare covers. These can include vision, dental, hearing, and even fitness programs. Part C plans also often have lower out-of-pocket costs compared to Original Medicare, providing financial relief for retirees and their families.

It is important to note that Medicare Advantage Plans have specific networks of doctors, hospitals, and other healthcare providers. This means that you may need to choose healthcare providers within the plan's network or pay higher costs for out-of-network services. However, some plans offer out-of-network coverage for emergencies or urgent care situations.

To enroll in a Medicare Advantage Plan, you must be eligible for Medicare Part A and Part B. Open enrollment for Medicare Advantage Plans occurs annually from October 15th to December 7th, during which you can switch plans or join a Part C plan for the first time. It's crucial to review your options and compare plans to find the one that best suits your healthcare needs and preferences.

In the following chapters, we will dive deeper into the various aspects of Medicare Advantage Plans, including the different types of plans available, how they work, and what to consider when selecting the right plan for you. We will also cover common questions and concerns often raised by retirees regarding coverage, costs, and restrictions.

By the end of this subchapter, you will have a solid understanding of Medicare Advantage Plans, enabling you to make informed decisions about your healthcare coverage and ensuring you receive the benefits you deserve.

Continue reading "Medicare Made Easy: Benefits for American Retirees" to explore the comprehensive information on Medicare prescription drug coverage, Medicare supplemental insurance options, Medicare coverage for preventive services, chronic disease management, mental health services, home healthcare services, skilled nursing facility care, hospice care, and durable medical equipment.

Remember, understanding Medicare Advantage Plans is a crucial step towards securing your health and well-being during your retirement years.

Benefits and Coverage of Medicare Advantage Plans

Medicare Advantage Plans, also known as Medicare Part C, are an alternative to Original Medicare (Part A and Part B) that offer additional benefits and coverage options. These plans are offered by private insurance companies approved by Medicare and provide all the benefits of Original Medicare, along with some extra perks. In this subchapter, we will delve into the benefits and coverage of Medicare Advantage Plans and how they can benefit retirees and their families.

One of the primary advantages of Medicare Advantage Plans is their comprehensive coverage. These plans often include prescription drug coverage (Part D), which can be a significant benefit for retirees who require regular medications. This means that you can get all your healthcare needs met under one plan, simplifying the process and reducing hassle.

Another key benefit of Medicare Advantage Plans is the potential for additional coverage beyond what Original Medicare offers. Many plans include benefits such as dental, vision, and hearing coverage, which are not covered by Original Medicare. This can be especially valuable for retirees and their families who may experience age-related changes in their oral, visual, or auditory health.

Medicare Advantage Plans also typically offer coverage for preventive services, chronic disease management, mental health services, home healthcare services, skilled nursing facility care, hospice care, and durable medical equipment. This wide range of coverage ensures that retirees have access to the care they need, regardless of their healthcare needs.

Additionally, Medicare Advantage Plans often have out-of-pocket maximums, which can provide financial peace of mind. This means that once you reach a certain limit on your medical expenses, your plan will cover the remaining costs for the year. This protection can be particularly beneficial for retirees who are on a fixed income and want to avoid unexpected healthcare expenses.

In conclusion, Medicare Advantage Plans offer retirees and their families a comprehensive and convenient way to receive healthcare coverage. With additional benefits such as prescription drug coverage, dental, vision, and hearing benefits, and coverage for preventive services and chronic disease management, these plans provide retirees with the peace of mind they deserve. By exploring the options available, retirees can find a Medicare Advantage Plan that suits their unique healthcare needs and helps them live a healthy and fulfilling retirement.

Enrollment and Disenrollment Periods

Understanding the enrollment and disenrollment periods is crucial for retirees and their families when it comes to navigating the complex world of Medicare. These periods determine when you can sign up for different parts of Medicare or make changes to your existing coverage. In this subchapter, we will delve into the various enrollment and disenrollment periods and their significance.

The Initial Enrollment Period (IEP) is the first opportunity for most individuals to enroll in Medicare. It typically begins three months before your 65th birthday and lasts for seven months. It is important to enroll during this period to avoid any late enrollment penalties and ensure that you have coverage when you need it.

Another important period is the Annual Enrollment Period (AEP), also known as the Open Enrollment Period. It occurs from October 15th to December 7th each year. During this time, retirees can make changes to their Medicare Advantage or prescription drug coverage. It is the perfect opportunity to review your current plan and compare it to other available options to ensure it still meets your needs.

Additionally, there are Special Enrollment Periods (SEPs) for those who experience certain life events, such as moving, losing employer coverage, or qualifying for Medicaid. SEPs provide flexibility outside of the standard enrollment periods and allow individuals to enroll or make changes to their coverage when they need it most.

On the other hand, the disenrollment period refers to the time when you can leave your Medicare Advantage plan and return to Original Medicare. The Medicare Advantage Disenrollment Period (MADP) runs from January 1st to February 14th. It offers an opportunity for those enrolled in a Medicare Advantage plan to switch back to Original Medicare and, if desired, sign up for a standalone prescription drug plan.

Understanding these enrollment and disenrollment periods is vital for retirees and their families as it allows them to make informed decisions regarding their Medicare coverage. By taking advantage of these periods, individuals can ensure they have the right plan for their needs and avoid any penalties or gaps in coverage.

In the following chapters, we will explore specific topics related to Medicare coverage, including prescription drug coverage, Medicare Advantage plans, supplemental insurance options, coverage for preventive services, chronic disease management, mental health services, home healthcare services, skilled nursing facility care, hospice care, and durable medical equipment. Stay tuned to gain a comprehensive understanding of each aspect of Medicare and make the most out of your retirement years.

Special Needs Plans (SNPs)

In this subchapter, we will explore Special Needs Plans (SNPs) and their benefits for retirees and their families. SNPs are a specialized type of Medicare Advantage plan that caters to individuals with specific health conditions or characteristics. If you or a loved one has unique healthcare needs, SNPs can provide tailored coverage and support.

SNPs are designed to provide comprehensive care for three main groups: individuals with chronic conditions, those who reside in institutions, and beneficiaries who are dual-eligible for both Medicare and Medicaid. These plans go beyond traditional Medicare coverage by offering additional benefits and services that address the specific needs of these populations.

For retirees with chronic conditions such as diabetes, heart disease, or cancer, a Chronic Condition SNP can be an excellent choice. These plans often include disease management programs, care coordination, and specialized healthcare providers who are knowledgeable about your specific condition. With a Chronic Condition SNP, you can receive the comprehensive care you need to manage your condition effectively.

Institutional SNPs are designed for retirees who reside in nursing homes, long-term care facilities, or other institutions. These plans provide coverage for the unique services required in these settings, including nursing care, therapy, and prescription medications. By enrolling in an Institutional SNP, you can ensure that your healthcare needs are met while residing in an institution.

Dual-Eligible SNPs are for individuals who qualify for both Medicare and Medicaid. These plans offer integrated coverage that combines the benefits of both programs. By enrolling in a Dual-Eligible SNP, you can simplify your healthcare coverage and access a wide range of services, including prescription drugs, hospital stays, and preventive care.

It's important to note that not all SNPs are available in every area, so it's essential to research the plans available in your location. To enroll in an SNP, you must meet the eligibility criteria specific to each plan.

SNPs can be a valuable option for retirees with unique healthcare needs. By choosing an SNP, you can access specialized care, disease management programs, and additional benefits that cater to your specific health condition or living situation. Consider exploring SNPs to find a plan that best meets your needs and ensures your peace of mind in retirement.

Chapter 5: Medicare Supplemental Insurance Options

Understanding Medicare Supplement Insurance (Medigap)

Medicare is a vital program that provides essential health coverage for American retirees. However, it is important to note that Medicare does not cover all healthcare expenses. This is where Medicare Supplement Insurance, also known as Medigap, comes into play. In this subchapter, we will delve into the details of Medigap and how it can benefit retirees and their families.

Medigap policies are private health insurance plans that help cover the gaps in Medicare coverage. These policies are sold by various insurance companies and can provide additional benefits such as coverage for copayments, coinsurance, and deductibles. It is important to understand that Medigap policies can only be purchased if you have Original Medicare (Part A and Part B).

One of the key advantages of Medigap is the flexibility it offers. Unlike Medicare Advantage plans, which replace Original Medicare, Medigap policies work alongside Original Medicare. This means you can choose your healthcare providers and visit any hospital or specialist who accepts Medicare patients.

Another notable benefit of Medigap is that it provides coverage for healthcare services when you travel outside of the United States. This can give retirees and their families peace of mind, knowing that they have coverage even when they are abroad.

It is crucial to understand that Medigap policies come with a premium, in addition to the premium paid for Part B coverage. However, the extra coverage provided by Medigap can help retirees save money in the long run by reducing out-of-pocket expenses.

When it comes to choosing a Medigap policy, it is essential to compare the available options and select the one that best suits your needs and budget. Medigap policies are standardized and labeled with letters (A, B, C, D, F, G, K, L, M, and N). Each lettered policy offers the same basic benefits, regardless of which insurance company is selling it. However, premiums may vary, so it is wise to shop around and compare prices.

In conclusion, Medicare Supplement Insurance (Medigap) is a valuable option for retirees and their families to bridge the gaps in Medicare coverage. By providing additional benefits and flexibility, Medigap policies can help alleviate financial burdens associated with healthcare expenses. When considering Medigap, it is crucial to research and compare policies to find the best fit for your individual needs.

Benefits and Coverage of Medigap Plans

Retirees and their families often find themselves overwhelmed when trying to navigate the complex world of Medicare. With so many options and coverage details to consider, it can be challenging to understand which plan is best suited to your needs. In this subchapter, we will explore the benefits and coverage of Medigap plans, providing you with the information you need to make an informed decision.

Medigap plans, also known as Medicare Supplement Insurance, are private insurance plans designed to help cover the gaps in Medicare coverage. These plans work alongside your Original Medicare (Parts A and B) to provide additional benefits, such as co-insurance, deductibles, and excess charges that are not covered by Medicare alone.

One of the key benefits of Medigap plans is the freedom to choose any doctor or hospital that accepts Medicare patients. This is important for retirees who want to maintain their relationship with their trusted healthcare providers. Medigap plans also offer coverage for services that Medicare does not fully cover, such as emergency medical care while traveling abroad.

Another advantage of Medigap plans is the peace of mind they provide. With a Medigap plan, you can rest easy knowing that unexpected medical expenses will be covered, reducing your out-of-pocket costs. This financial protection can be especially valuable for retirees on a fixed income.

Coverage options within Medigap plans can vary, so it's essential to understand what each plan offers. Plan benefits range from basic coverage to comprehensive coverage, allowing you to choose the option that best fits your needs and budget. Some plans may include additional benefits, such as coverage for prescription drugs or preventive services. It's crucial to carefully review the details of each plan to ensure it aligns with your specific healthcare requirements.

Medigap plans can be a valuable addition to your Medicare coverage, providing enhanced benefits and financial protection. By understanding the benefits and coverage options available, you can make an informed decision that best meets your healthcare needs as a retiree.

In the following chapters, we will delve deeper into other important aspects of Medicare, including prescription drug coverage, Medicare Advantage plans, supplemental insurance options, coverage for preventive services, chronic disease management, mental health services, home healthcare services, skilled nursing facility care, hospice care, and coverage for durable medical equipment. By exploring each topic thoroughly, we aim to empower you with the knowledge needed to navigate the Medicare system confidently.

Comparison of Medigap Plans

One of the key decisions retirees and their families face when it comes to Medicare is choosing the right Medigap plan. Medigap plans, also known as Medicare Supplement Insurance, help cover the gaps in Medicare coverage, such as deductibles, copayments, and coinsurance. With several different Medigap plans available, it's important to understand the options and compare them to make an informed decision.

Plan Comparison: Medigap plans are standardized across most states, which means that the benefits offered by each plan are the same, regardless of the insurance company offering it. However, the prices may vary, so it's essential to compare the premiums and costs associated with each plan. The plans are labeled with letters from A to N, with each letter representing a different set of benefits. For example, Plan A offers the basic benefits, while Plan F provides the most comprehensive coverage.

Coverage Options: When comparing Medigap plans, it's crucial to consider your specific healthcare needs. Some plans may offer coverage for services that others don't. For instance, Plan G covers Medicare Part B excess charges, which can be important if you frequently see doctors who don't accept Medicare assignment. Plan N, on the other hand, requires copayments for certain services but generally has lower premiums.

Cost Considerations: Medigap plans come with monthly premiums, in addition to the premiums for Part B of Medicare. It's important to evaluate the premium costs and compare them with the potential out-of-pocket expenses you may incur without a Medigap plan. Balancing the monthly costs with the potential benefits and coverage can help you determine the most cost-effective option for your situation.

Enrollment Period: It's crucial to be aware of the Medigap Open Enrollment Period. This period begins when you turn 65 and enroll in Medicare Part B. During this period, insurance companies are required to sell you any Medigap plan they offer, regardless of your health condition. If you miss this period, you may still be eligible for a Medigap plan, but insurance companies may charge higher premiums or deny coverage based on your health.

Consulting an Expert: Choosing the right Medigap plan can be a complex process. Consulting with a licensed insurance agent or a Medicare expert can help retirees and their families navigate the options, understand the costs, and make an informed decision based on their individual needs.

In conclusion, understanding and comparing Medigap plans is essential for retirees and their families to ensure they have adequate coverage for their healthcare needs. By considering the plan benefits, coverage options, costs, and consulting with experts, retirees can make an informed decision and secure the best Medigap plan that suits their individual needs and budgets.

Open Enrollment and Guaranteed Issue Rights

As retirees and their families navigate the complex world of Medicare, it is crucial to understand the concepts of open enrollment and guaranteed issue rights. These two aspects play a significant role in ensuring that you receive the best possible healthcare coverage and benefits.

Open enrollment refers to a specific time period each year when you can make changes to your Medicare coverage. It typically runs from October 15th to December 7th, allowing you to switch between Original Medicare, Medicare Advantage plans, and Medicare prescription drug coverage. During this period, you have the freedom to explore different options and select a plan that best suits your needs.

One key benefit of open enrollment is that it provides an opportunity to review and modify your coverage. Perhaps you have experienced changes in your health or medication needs, or maybe you feel that your current plan no longer meets your expectations. Open enrollment allows you to make adjustments and ensure that your healthcare needs are adequately addressed.

On the other hand, guaranteed issue rights protect individuals who may have pre-existing conditions or face other circumstances that could result in denial of coverage. These rights ensure that insurance companies cannot refuse to sell you a Medicare supplement insurance plan, also known as Medigap, based on your health status or charge you higher premiums due to existing health conditions.

Guaranteed issue rights are triggered during specific situations, such as when you lose your current coverage, move out of your plan's service area, or if your plan no longer offers coverage in your area. In these cases, insurance companies are required to offer you a Medigap policy without any exclusions or waiting periods. This is particularly important for retirees who may have pre-existing conditions or require ongoing medical care.

Understanding open enrollment and guaranteed issue rights is essential for retirees and their families to make informed decisions about their Medicare coverage. By taking advantage of open enrollment, you can reassess your needs and make changes to your plan. Additionally, guaranteed issue rights provide peace of mind, ensuring that you have access to the coverage you need, regardless of your health status.

In conclusion, open enrollment and guaranteed issue rights are critical components of Medicare coverage for retirees and their families. These provisions offer the flexibility to evaluate and modify your plan during a specific time period and protect individuals with pre-existing conditions from being denied coverage. By familiarizing yourself with these concepts, you can navigate the Medicare system with confidence and ensure that you receive the best possible healthcare benefits.

Chapter 6: Medicare Coverage for Preventive Services

Importance of Preventive Services for Retirees

As retirees embark on a new chapter of their lives, it becomes increasingly important to prioritize their health and well-being. This subchapter will shed light on the significance of preventive services for retirees and the benefits they can bring to their lives. By understanding the value of preventive care, retirees and their families can make informed decisions about their healthcare needs.

Medicare, the federal health insurance program for Americans aged 65 and older, offers a range of preventive services that are specifically tailored to meet the needs of retirees. These services are designed to detect and prevent potential health issues before they become more severe or costly to treat. By taking advantage of these preventive services, retirees can not only maintain their health but also potentially extend their quality of life.

One of the key benefits of preventive care is early detection. Regular screenings and check-ups can help identify potential health concerns such as cancer, diabetes, cardiovascular diseases, and osteoporosis at an early stage when they are easier to manage and treat. This can significantly improve the chances of successful treatment and reduce the risk of complications.

Furthermore, preventive services can play a crucial role in managing chronic diseases. Medicare provides coverage for chronic disease management, offering services such as diabetes self-management training, cardiovascular disease screenings, and personalized care plans. By actively managing their chronic conditions, retirees can better control their symptoms, improve their quality of life, and potentially reduce the need for more intensive medical interventions.

Mental health is another essential aspect of overall well-being. Medicare recognizes the importance of mental health services and covers a wide range of preventive and treatment services for mental health conditions. This includes screenings for depression and anxiety, counseling services, and access to psychiatrists and psychologists. Prioritizing mental health can help retirees maintain their cognitive function, emotional well-being, and overall quality of life.

In addition to preventive care for physical and mental health, Medicare also covers preventive services in home healthcare settings, skilled nursing facilities, and hospice care. These services are designed to meet the specific needs of retirees who may require additional support due to age-related or chronic conditions. By providing access to necessary care and support, Medicare aims to enhance the overall well-being of retirees and improve their quality of life.

In conclusion, the importance of preventive services for retirees cannot be overstated. By taking advantage of the preventive care options available through Medicare, retirees can actively protect and manage their health. Regular screenings, check-ups, and disease management programs can lead to early detection, better control of chronic conditions, and ultimately a higher quality of life for retirees. It is crucial for retirees and their families to educate themselves about the preventive services offered by Medicare to make informed decisions about their healthcare needs. By prioritizing preventive care, retirees can ensure a healthier and more fulfilling retirement journey.

Preventive Services Covered by Medicare

As retirees and their families, it is essential to understand the comprehensive benefits provided by Medicare. One crucial aspect of

Medicare coverage is the inclusion of preventive services. These services are designed to detect potential health issues before they become more severe and to promote overall well-being.

Medicare covers a range of preventive services to ensure that you can maintain good health and prevent the onset of chronic conditions. Under Medicare, you are entitled to receive a variety of screenings, vaccinations, and counseling services at no additional cost to you.

Preventive screenings covered by Medicare include mammograms, colonoscopies, and screenings for prostate cancer, diabetes, and cardiovascular diseases. These screenings are vital in detecting conditions early on when they are more treatable and manageable.

In addition to screenings, Medicare covers vaccinations to protect against diseases such as influenza, pneumonia, and hepatitis B. Staying up to date on vaccinations is crucial in preventing the spread of infectious diseases, especially for older adults who may be more susceptible.

Medicare also offers counseling services to help retirees manage their health effectively. These services include nutrition counseling, smoking cessation counseling, and annual wellness visits. These counseling sessions aim to provide guidance on maintaining a healthy lifestyle, managing chronic conditions, and preventing the onset of new health issues.

By taking advantage of these preventive services, you can actively participate in managing your health and well-being. Regular screenings, vaccinations, and counseling sessions can help you stay proactive in preventing diseases and maintaining a high quality of life.

It's important to note that while Medicare covers many preventive services, it's always recommended to consult with your healthcare provider to determine which services are appropriate for you based on your age, gender, and medical history.

As retirees, taking care of your health should be a top priority. With Medicare's coverage for preventive services, you can ensure that you have access to the necessary screenings, vaccinations, and counseling sessions to maintain your well-being and enjoy your retirement years to the fullest. Stay proactive, stay healthy!

Annual Wellness Visit and Personalized Prevention Plan

As retirees, it is important to prioritize your health and well-being to ensure a fulfilling and active retirement. Medicare offers various benefits and services that can help you maintain good health and prevent potential illnesses. One such benefit is the Annual Wellness Visit and Personalized Prevention Plan, designed to provide you with a comprehensive evaluation of your health status and offer personalized recommendations for preventive care.

The Annual Wellness Visit is a yearly appointment with your primary care physician to discuss your overall health and create a personalized prevention plan. During this visit, your doctor will review your medical history, inquire about any current health concerns, and conduct a series of screenings and assessments to evaluate your risk for certain diseases and conditions. This comprehensive evaluation serves as a foundation for developing a personalized prevention plan tailored to your specific needs.

The Personalized Prevention Plan includes recommendations for preventive services and screenings that are covered by Medicare. These services may include vaccinations, cancer screenings, cardiovascular assessments, diabetes screenings, and more. By following the recommendations outlined in your prevention plan, you can stay ahead of potential health issues and take proactive steps to maintain optimal health.

The Annual Wellness Visit and Personalized Prevention Plan are crucial in preventing and managing chronic diseases. By identifying risk factors and implementing preventive measures, you can reduce the likelihood of developing serious health conditions such as diabetes, heart disease, and certain cancers. This proactive approach not only improves your quality of life but also helps to minimize healthcare costs associated with treating chronic diseases.

Additionally, Medicare coverage for preventive services extends beyond the Annual Wellness Visit. Medicare offers coverage for various preventive screenings, tests, and vaccines that can help identify and prevent potential health issues before they become more serious. From mammograms and colonoscopies to flu shots and smoking cessation counseling, Medicare provides a wide range of preventive services to keep you healthy and active.

In conclusion, the Annual Wellness Visit and Personalized Prevention Plan are essential components of Medicare benefits for American retirees. By taking advantage of these services, you can prioritize your health, identify potential health risks, and take proactive steps to prevent and manage chronic diseases. Medicare coverage for preventive services further enhances your ability to maintain good health and enjoy a fulfilling retirement. Remember, your health is your greatest asset, and Medicare is here to support you every step of the way.

Chapter 7: Medicare Coverage for Chronic Disease Management

Common Chronic Diseases among Retirees

As retirees and their families enter a new phase of life, it is important to be aware of the common chronic diseases that may arise during this stage. Chronic diseases can significantly impact one's quality of life and can place a burden on both physical and financial aspects. In this subchapter, we will explore the most prevalent chronic diseases among retirees and how Medicare can provide benefits and coverage for managing these conditions.

One of the most common chronic diseases among retirees is cardiovascular disease. This includes conditions such as high blood pressure, heart disease, and stroke. Medicare provides coverage for preventive services such as blood pressure screenings and cholesterol checks to help manage and prevent cardiovascular diseases.

Another prevalent chronic disease is diabetes. Diabetes can lead to various complications if not properly managed. Medicare offers coverage for diabetes screenings, supplies, and self-management training to ensure retirees have the necessary tools to keep their condition under control.

Arthritis is another chronic disease that affects many retirees. This condition can cause joint pain and stiffness, making it challenging to perform daily activities. Medicare covers treatments such as physical therapy, occupational therapy, and medications to alleviate symptoms and improve mobility.

Mental health conditions, such as depression and anxiety, are also common among retirees. Medicare provides coverage for mental health services, including counseling and therapy sessions. It is important to prioritize mental well-being alongside physical health during retirement.

In addition to the above chronic diseases, retirees may also face conditions such as respiratory diseases, osteoporosis, and cancer. Medicare offers coverage for treatments, medications, and screenings related to these conditions, ensuring retirees have access to necessary care.

It is important for retirees and their families to understand the various Medicare options available to them. Medicare Advantage plans, Medicare supplemental insurance options, and Medicare prescription drug coverage can provide additional benefits and coverage for managing chronic diseases. These plans often include services such as preventive care, prescription medications, and specialist visits.

By being aware of the common chronic diseases among retirees and understanding the Medicare coverage options, retirees and their families can make informed decisions about their healthcare. Medicare is designed to provide comprehensive coverage and support for managing chronic diseases, ensuring retirees can lead healthy and fulfilling lives during their retirement years.

Medicare Coverage for Chronic Disease Management

Living with a chronic disease can be challenging, but with the right support and resources, managing your condition becomes more manageable. In this subchapter, we will explore how Medicare provides coverage for chronic disease management, ensuring you receive the care and support you need to lead a fulfilling life during your retirement years.

Medicare understands the importance of managing chronic diseases, such as diabetes, heart disease, and arthritis, to maintain your overall health and well-being. That's why it offers a range of coverage options to help you navigate through the complexities of chronic disease management.

One of the key benefits Medicare offers is coverage for doctor visits and medical services related to the management of chronic diseases. This includes regular check-ups, consultations with specialists, and diagnostic tests. Medicare also covers medications prescribed for chronic conditions, ensuring you have access to the necessary treatment to control your disease effectively.

Furthermore, Medicare provides coverage for disease management programs, such as diabetes self-management training and cardiac rehabilitation. These programs offer education, guidance, and support to help you better understand your condition and develop strategies for self-care. By participating in these programs, you can learn how to monitor your health, make lifestyle changes, and adhere to your treatment plan, leading to improved outcomes and a higher quality of life.

In addition to medical services and disease management programs, Medicare also covers certain medical equipment and supplies necessary for chronic disease management. This includes items like blood glucose monitors, insulin pumps, and mobility aids, helping you effectively manage your condition at home.

It is important to note that certain Medicare Advantage plans may offer additional benefits and resources tailored to chronic disease management. These plans often include care coordination services, access to specialized care networks, and personalized support from care managers. If you have a chronic condition, exploring Medicare Advantage plans may provide you with comprehensive coverage and additional resources to support your specific needs.

Managing a chronic disease doesn't have to be overwhelming. Medicare is here to support you every step of the way, from coverage for medical services and medications to disease management programs and specialized care options. By utilizing the resources available, you can take charge of your health and enjoy a fulfilling and active retirement.

Disease Management Programs and Resources

As retirees and their families, it is important to understand the various resources available to you when it comes to managing diseases and maintaining your health. Medicare offers a range of programs and resources that can provide support and assistance in dealing with chronic conditions and ensuring you receive the appropriate care.

One of the key aspects of disease management is access to necessary medications. Medicare prescription drug coverage, also known as Part D, helps you afford the medications you need to manage your conditions. This coverage can be obtained through standalone prescription drug plans or through Medicare Advantage plans, which offer comprehensive coverage that includes both medical services and prescription drugs.

Medicare Advantage plans are an alternative to Original Medicare and provide additional benefits, such as vision, dental, and hearing coverage. These plans are particularly beneficial for retirees as they often offer disease management programs that focus on specific conditions like diabetes or heart disease. These programs typically provide personalized support, education, and resources to help you effectively manage your condition and improve your overall well-being.

In addition to prescription drug coverage and Medicare Advantage plans, there are other options available to enhance your Medicare coverage. Medicare supplemental insurance, also known as Medigap, can help cover the out-of-pocket costs associated with Original Medicare, such as deductibles, copayments, and coinsurance. This additional coverage can provide peace of mind and ensure you have the financial support you need for managing chronic conditions.

Furthermore, Medicare covers a wide range of preventive services to help you stay healthy. These services include vaccinations, screenings, and counseling for various diseases and conditions. Regular preventive care can help detect potential health issues early on and prevent the development of more serious conditions.

In addition to physical health, Medicare also recognizes the importance of mental health. Coverage for mental health services includes counseling, therapy, and inpatient care if necessary. Mental health is an essential component of overall well-being, and Medicare ensures that retirees have access to the care they need.

Home healthcare services, skilled nursing facility care, and hospice care are also covered by Medicare under certain conditions. These services provide important support for individuals who require assistance with daily activities or are in need of specialized care due to a chronic condition or terminal illness.

Lastly, Medicare covers durable medical equipment such as wheelchairs, walkers, and oxygen equipment. These resources can greatly improve your quality of life and mobility, allowing you to manage your condition more effectively.

In conclusion, Medicare offers a comprehensive range of programs and resources to support retirees and their families in managing diseases and maintaining their health. From prescription drug coverage and disease management programs to coverage for preventive services, mental health, and specialized care, Medicare ensures that you have the necessary support and resources to lead a healthy and fulfilling retirement.

Chapter 8: Medicare Coverage for Mental Health Services

Mental Health and Aging

As we age, it is important to prioritize not only our physical health but also our mental well-being. In this subchapter, we will explore the significance of mental health in the aging process and how Medicare can support retirees and their families in accessing the necessary services.

Aging can bring about various life changes, such as retirement, loss of loved ones, and declining physical health, which can impact mental health. It is essential to recognize the symptoms of mental health conditions, such as depression, anxiety, and dementia, as they can significantly affect the quality of life and overall health of older adults.

Medicare, the federal health insurance program for retirees, provides coverage for a range of mental health services. This includes outpatient counseling and therapy sessions with licensed mental health professionals. Whether you are seeking help for depression, grief, or simply adjusting to life changes, Medicare can help you access the necessary support.

Additionally, Medicare offers coverage for mental health screenings, which can be crucial in identifying any potential issues early on. Regular screenings can ensure that any mental health concerns are detected and addressed promptly, leading to better outcomes and improved well-being.

Furthermore, Medicare covers prescription medications, including those prescribed for mental health conditions. This coverage extends to Medicare Part D, the prescription drug coverage program. If you require medication to manage mental health conditions, Medicare can help alleviate the financial burden by providing access to affordable prescription drugs.

For those who wish to explore additional mental health services, Medicare Advantage plans are available. These plans, offered by private insurance companies approved by Medicare, often include coverage for mental health services not covered under traditional Medicare. They may also provide access to wellness programs, counseling, and other resources to support mental well-being.

In conclusion, mental health is an integral part of overall well-being, especially as we age. Medicare recognizes the importance of mental health services and offers coverage for counseling, therapy, screenings, and prescription medications. Additionally, Medicare Advantage plans provide further options for retirees and their families to access comprehensive mental health support. Prioritizing mental health is essential for enjoying a fulfilling and healthy retirement, and Medicare is here to support you every step of the way.

Medicare Coverage for Mental Health Services

As retirees, it's important to prioritize our mental well-being just as much as our physical health. Fortunately, Medicare provides coverage for a wide range of mental health services, ensuring that you have access to the care you need. In this subchapter, we will explore the various aspects of Medicare coverage for mental health services and how you can make the most of these benefits.

Under Medicare, mental health services are covered under Part B, which includes outpatient services. This means that you can receive mental health treatment from licensed professionals such as psychiatrists, psychologists, and clinical social workers. These professionals are qualified to diagnose and treat mental health conditions, helping you manage and improve your mental well-being.

Medicare covers a range of mental health services, including therapy sessions, counseling, and diagnostic screenings. These services can be instrumental in addressing conditions such as depression, anxiety, bipolar disorder, and schizophrenia. Medicare also covers partial hospitalization programs, which provide intensive outpatient treatment for individuals who require more structured care but do not need to be hospitalized.

Additionally, Medicare covers prescription medications for mental health conditions under Part D. This means that you can access necessary antidepressants, antipsychotics, and other medications prescribed by your mental health provider at an affordable cost. It's important to review your specific Part D plan to ensure that your prescribed medications are covered.

To make the most of your Medicare coverage for mental health services, it's essential to be proactive in seeking the care you need. Start by finding a mental health provider who accepts Medicare assignment, as this ensures that you pay the least out-of-pocket costs. You can search for such providers through the Medicare website or by calling their helpline.

Remember that Medicare also covers annual wellness visits, during which you can discuss your mental health concerns with your primary care physician. These visits provide an opportunity for early detection, prevention, and treatment of mental health conditions. It's crucial to communicate openly with your healthcare provider about any symptoms or concerns you may have.

In conclusion, Medicare provides comprehensive coverage for mental health services, allowing retirees to prioritize their mental well-being. By understanding the coverage available and being proactive in seeking care, you can ensure that you receive the necessary support to maintain a healthy and fulfilling retirement. Take advantage of these benefits and prioritize your mental health today.

Counseling and Therapy Services

As you navigate the complexities of retirement, it's important to remember that your mental and emotional well-being are just as crucial as your physical health. Medicare understands this and provides coverage for counseling and therapy services to help you maintain a positive and fulfilling life during your golden years.

Under Medicare, you have access to various counseling and therapy services, including individual counseling, family therapy, and group therapy. These services aim to address a range of mental health concerns, such as anxiety, depression, grief, and relationship issues. Additionally, Medicare covers therapy for managing chronic conditions, such as diabetes or heart disease, which often come with emotional challenges.

It's important to note that Medicare covers these services when they are provided by qualified professionals, such as psychologists, clinical social workers, and licensed professional counselors. To ensure you receive the best care, it's essential to choose providers who accept Medicare assignment.

Moreover, Medicare covers mental health services both in outpatient and inpatient settings. This means that whether you prefer individual therapy sessions in a clinic or group therapy sessions in a hospital, you can find the care that suits your needs.

Furthermore, Medicare also covers counseling and therapy services provided through telehealth. This option allows you to receive mental health care from the comfort of your own home, eliminating the need for travel or waiting rooms. Telehealth services have become increasingly popular, especially during the COVID-19 pandemic, and Medicare ensures that you have access to this convenient and safe option.

Taking care of your mental health is an essential part of living a fulfilling retirement. Medicare recognizes this and provides coverage for counseling and therapy services to support your emotional well-being. Whether you're dealing with grief, anxiety, or chronic disease management, Medicare ensures that you have access to qualified professionals who can help you navigate these challenges.

Remember, your mental health matters, and with Medicare, you can receive the support you need to lead a happy and healthy life during your retirement years. Don't hesitate to explore the counseling and therapy services available to you under Medicare – they are here to help you every step of the way.

Chapter 9: Medicare Coverage for Home Healthcare Services

Home Healthcare Services for Retirees

As we age, the need for healthcare services becomes increasingly important. For retirees, it's essential to have access to quality care that allows them to maintain their independence and receive the support they need in the comfort of their own homes. In this subchapter, we will explore the various home healthcare services available to retirees and how Medicare can help cover these costs.

Home healthcare services encompass a range of medical and non-medical assistance provided in a retiree's home. These services can include skilled nursing care, physical therapy, occupational therapy, speech therapy, and even personal care assistance. The goal of home healthcare is to promote wellness, manage chronic conditions, and ensure a safe living environment for retirees.

Medicare, the federal health insurance program for people aged 65 and older, offers coverage for many home healthcare services. Under Medicare Part A, eligible retirees can receive skilled nursing care, home health aide services, and certain therapy services if they meet specific criteria. This coverage is typically provided on a short-term basis, such as after a hospital stay or for a specific medical condition.

For retirees who require ongoing home healthcare services, Medicare Part B can help cover expenses such as physical therapy, occupational therapy, and speech therapy. Additionally, Medicare Part B can also cover durable medical equipment, such as wheelchairs or oxygen tanks, needed for home use.

It's important to note that Medicare does not cover 24-hour home care or assistance with activities of daily living, such as bathing or dressing, unless it is provided as part of skilled nursing care. However, there may be other options available to retirees, such as long-term care insurance or Medicaid, which can help cover these services.

To access home healthcare services, retirees must meet certain criteria, including being homebound and requiring skilled nursing care or therapy services. A doctor's order is necessary to initiate these services, and the care must be provided by a Medicare-certified home health agency.

In conclusion, home healthcare services are an invaluable resource for retirees who wish to age in place and maintain their independence. Medicare offers coverage for a wide range of home healthcare services, including skilled nursing care, therapy services, and durable medical equipment. However, it's important to understand the limitations of Medicare coverage and explore other options if additional assistance is required. By taking advantage of these services, retirees can receive the care they need in the comfort of their own homes, promoting overall wellness and quality of life.

Medicare Coverage for Home Health Services

As retirees and their families navigate the complexities of Medicare, understanding the coverage options available for home health services is crucial. Medicare provides coverage for a range of care provided in the comfort of your own home, ensuring that you receive the necessary support without the need for hospitalization or institutional care.

Home health services encompass a wide array of medical and non-medical assistance, including skilled nursing care, therapy services, and personal care services. If you qualify for Medicare, you may be eligible for coverage of these services under certain conditions.

To be eligible for Medicare coverage for home health services, you must meet specific criteria. Firstly, you must be under the care of a doctor who has certified your need for skilled nursing care or therapy services. Additionally, you must be homebound, meaning it is difficult for you to leave your home without the assistance of another person or medical equipment.

Under Medicare Part A, you are entitled to coverage for home health services if you are already enrolled in Medicare and meet the eligibility requirements. Medicare Part A covers skilled nursing care, physical therapy, occupational therapy, speech-language pathology services, and certain medical supplies.

It is important to note that Medicare coverage for home health services is not intended to provide long-term care or custodial care. Instead, it focuses on short-term, intermittent care that is medically necessary and aimed at improving your health or maintaining your current condition.

In addition to Medicare Part A coverage, you may also be eligible for coverage under Medicare Part B. Part B covers medically necessary services and supplies, including doctor's visits, outpatient care, and preventive services. If you require home health services that are not covered under Part A, Part B may provide the necessary coverage.

Understanding the coverage options available for home health services is essential for retirees and their families. By familiarizing yourself with the eligibility criteria and the types of services covered, you can ensure that you receive the care you need while maximizing your Medicare benefits.

In the next subchapters, we will explore other aspects of Medicare coverage that are relevant to retirees and their families. These include Medicare coverage for skilled nursing facility care, hospice care, mental health services, and durable medical equipment, among others. By delving into these topics, you will gain a comprehensive understanding of the benefits that Medicare offers and how they can support your healthcare needs in retirement.

Qualifications and Limitations for Home Health Care

As retirees and their families navigate the complexities of Medicare, it is essential to understand the qualifications and limitations for home health care services. Home health care offers a convenient and cost-effective option for individuals who require medical assistance but prefer to receive care in the comfort of their own homes. In this subchapter, we will explore the eligibility criteria, coverage, and limitations associated with Medicare's home health care services.

To qualify for Medicare-covered home health care, individuals must meet specific criteria. Firstly, you must be enrolled in Medicare Part A and/or Part B. Secondly, your doctor must certify that you require skilled nursing care or therapy services on an intermittent basis. These services should be necessary to treat a condition or illness, and it must be reasonable to expect that your condition will improve with these services. Additionally, you must be homebound, meaning it is challenging for you to leave your home without assistance due to your medical condition.

Medicare's home health care coverage includes a range of services provided by skilled professionals such as nurses, physical therapists, occupational therapists, and speech-language pathologists. These services may include wound care, medication management, physical rehabilitation, and assistance with activities of daily living. Medicare also covers medical supplies, durable medical equipment, and certain home health aide services on a limited basis.

It is important to note that while home health care can be a valuable resource, it has certain limitations. Medicare's coverage for home health care is typically time-limited and intermittent. Medicare will cover skilled nursing care and therapy services for a limited period, usually up to 28 hours per week, for a maximum of 60 days. However, in exceptional cases, this coverage can be extended. Additionally, Medicare does not cover 24-hour care or personal care services that are not related to your medical condition.

Understanding the qualifications and limitations of home health care under Medicare is crucial for retirees and their families. It allows you to make informed decisions about your healthcare options and plan for any additional costs or services that may be required. By working closely with your healthcare providers and understanding your Medicare benefits, you can access the necessary care while maximizing the benefits available to you.

Chapter 10: Medicare Coverage for Skilled Nursing Facility Care

Understanding Skilled Nursing Facility (SNF) Care

When it comes to your healthcare needs, it's important to understand all the options available to you. One such option is Skilled Nursing Facility (SNF) care, which is covered by Medicare. In this subchapter, we will delve into what SNF care entails and how it can benefit you or your loved ones.

Skilled Nursing Facility (SNF) care refers to the specialized care provided by trained medical professionals in a facility, typically following a hospital stay. It is designed for individuals who require intense rehabilitation or medical care that cannot be provided at home. SNFs offer round-the-clock nursing care, physical therapy, occupational therapy, speech therapy, and other related services.

Medicare covers SNF care under certain conditions. To be eligible, you must have had a qualifying hospital stay of at least three consecutive days, and your doctor must determine that you need daily skilled care that can only be provided in a SNF setting. Medicare will cover up to 100 days of SNF care per benefit period, with the first 20 days covered in full and a daily coinsurance for days 21-100.

It's important to note that SNF care is different from long-term care. Medicare does not cover long-term care in a SNF if it is solely for custodial care (assistance with activities of daily living) and not for skilled care. However, if you meet the requirements for skilled care, Medicare will cover your stay in a SNF.

SNF care can be a crucial step in your recovery process. It allows you to receive specialized care and therapy in a supportive environment, ensuring that you regain your independence and achieve the highest level of functioning possible. The skilled nursing staff will work closely with your healthcare team to develop a personalized care plan tailored to your specific needs.

In summary, Skilled Nursing Facility (SNF) care is an important benefit provided by Medicare for individuals who require intense rehabilitation or medical care following a hospital stay. It offers specialized services and round-the-clock nursing care to help you recover and regain independence. Understanding the eligibility requirements and coverage limitations will help you make informed decisions about your healthcare needs.

Medicare Coverage for SNF Care

As retirees and their families navigate the complexities of healthcare, understanding the Medicare coverage for skilled nursing facility (SNF) care becomes crucial. In this subchapter, we will explore the benefits and guidelines for accessing SNF care under Medicare, ensuring that you make informed decisions for your loved ones' long-term care needs.

Skilled nursing facility care refers to the specialized services provided by trained healthcare professionals in a facility, usually after a hospital stay. Medicare Part A covers a portion of the costs associated with SNF care, provided certain conditions are met.

To qualify for Medicare coverage for SNF care, you must have a qualifying hospital stay of at least three consecutive days. Following this, you are eligible for up to 100 days of SNF care, with Medicare covering the costs for the first 20 days in full, and a daily copayment for days 21 to 100.

It is important to note that Medicare covers skilled care services, such as nursing care, physical therapy, occupational therapy, and speech-language pathology services. However, it does not cover custodial care, such as assistance with activities of daily living (ADLs) like bathing, dressing, and eating.

Before entering a skilled nursing facility, it is essential to understand the criteria for Medicare coverage. The care must be provided by a Medicare-certified facility, and a doctor must certify that it is medically necessary for you to receive skilled care on a daily basis. Additionally, your condition must show improvement potential or require skilled nursing or therapy services to maintain your current condition.

It is also important to be aware of Medicare's guidelines around the timing of SNF care. Medicare coverage for SNF care begins within 30 days of a hospital stay and requires admission to a Medicare-certified SNF within that timeframe.

Understanding the nuances of Medicare coverage for SNF care can significantly impact your long-term care planning. By being aware of the qualifying criteria, the specific services covered, and the timing requirements, you can make informed decisions about the best course of action for you or your loved one's healthcare needs.

In the next section, we will delve into Medicare coverage for hospice care, providing you with a comprehensive understanding of the benefits available for end-of-life care.

Qualifications and Limitations for SNF Care

Skilled Nursing Facility (SNF) care is an essential benefit provided by Medicare for eligible individuals who require specialized care and rehabilitation services after a hospital stay. This subchapter aims to provide retirees and their families with a comprehensive understanding of the qualifications and limitations associated with SNF care under Medicare.

To qualify for SNF care, you must meet certain criteria. Firstly, you must have been admitted to a hospital for a minimum of three consecutive days, excluding the day of discharge. Additionally, your doctor must certify that you require daily skilled nursing care or skilled rehabilitation services, which can only be provided in a SNF.

Medicare covers up to 100 days of SNF care per benefit period. However, it is important to note that Medicare will only cover the full cost for the first 20 days. From day 21 to day 100, a daily coinsurance amount will be required. It is crucial to review your specific Medicare plan to understand the coinsurance amount you will be responsible for during this period.

Furthermore, to receive Medicare coverage for SNF care, you must choose a SNF that is Medicare-certified. It is advisable to consult with your doctor or a Medicare counselor to ensure that the SNF you choose meets the necessary requirements.

It is important to be aware of the limitations associated with SNF care under Medicare. Medicare will only cover skilled nursing and rehabilitation services provided by certified professionals. Any custodial care, such as assistance with activities of daily living (ADLs) like bathing or dressing, will not be covered. Additionally, Medicare does not cover long-term stays in a SNF, and therefore, it is essential to plan accordingly.

Understanding the qualifications and limitations of SNF care can help retirees and their families make informed decisions regarding their healthcare needs. It is advisable to review your Medicare plan and discuss your options with healthcare professionals to ensure you receive appropriate care while maximizing your Medicare benefits.

This subchapter provides retirees and their families with valuable information on Medicare coverage for skilled nursing facility care. It is crucial to consider this information alongside other chapters in this book, such as Medicare coverage for chronic disease management, preventive services, and home healthcare services, to gain a comprehensive understanding of the benefits available to you as a Medicare beneficiary.

Chapter 11: Medicare Coverage for Hospice Care

Importance of Hospice Care for End-of-Life Support

When facing the end of life, it is important to have access to comprehensive care that focuses on providing comfort, dignity, and support. Hospice care is a specialized form of healthcare that offers this vital support to individuals and their families during the final stages of life. This subchapter explores the importance of hospice care for end-of-life support, highlighting the benefits it brings to retirees and their families.

Hospice care is covered by Medicare, making it an accessible and affordable option for American retirees. It provides a range of services, including pain management, emotional and spiritual support, and assistance with daily tasks. These services are delivered by a team of healthcare professionals, including doctors, nurses, social workers, and spiritual counselors, who work together to ensure the highest quality of care.

One of the key benefits of hospice care is its focus on improving the quality of life for individuals during their final days. Hospice teams are trained to provide personalized care that addresses the unique needs and preferences of each patient. They work closely with the individual and their family to develop a care plan that respects their wishes, promotes comfort, and provides emotional support.

In addition to physical and emotional care, hospice care also offers support to the families of individuals nearing the end of life. It can be an incredibly challenging and emotional time for loved ones, and hospice care provides guidance, counseling, and bereavement services to help them navigate this difficult journey.

Choosing hospice care at the end of life is a decision that requires careful consideration. It is important for retirees and their families to understand the benefits and options available to them through Medicare. By researching and understanding the coverage and services provided under Medicare, retirees can make informed decisions about their end-of-life care.

In conclusion, hospice care plays a crucial role in providing comprehensive support to individuals and their families during the end of life. It offers comfort, dignity, and emotional support, ensuring that retirees receive the care they need and deserve. By utilizing Medicare benefits for hospice care, retirees can access these essential services and focus on what truly matters during their final days.

Medicare Coverage for Hospice Care

When faced with a terminal illness, Medicare provides coverage for hospice care to ensure that patients receive the necessary support and comfort during their final days. Hospice care focuses on improving the quality of life for those with a life-limiting illness, rather than curative treatments.

Medicare covers hospice care through Medicare Part A, which includes a wide range of services tailored to meet the needs of the patient and their family. These services encompass medical, emotional, and spiritual support, ensuring that the patient's physical symptoms are managed effectively while also addressing their emotional and spiritual well-being.

Under Medicare, hospice care can be received in various settings, including the patient's home, nursing homes, and specialized hospice facilities. This flexibility allows patients to choose the environment in which they feel most comfortable and supported.

Medicare covers a comprehensive set of services related to hospice care, such as doctor visits, nursing care, medical equipment and supplies, prescription drugs for pain relief and symptom management, and even short-term hospital stays if necessary. Additionally, Medicare also covers counseling services for both the patient and their family members to help them cope with the emotional challenges that may arise during this difficult time.

It is important for retirees and their families to understand that in order to qualify for Medicare's hospice care coverage, the patient must have a life expectancy of six months or less, as certified by their doctor. However, if the patient's condition improves or their illness goes into remission, they may no longer be eligible for hospice care and would instead resume their regular Medicare coverage.

Medicare's coverage for hospice care is designed to provide comfort and support to patients and their families during a challenging time. It ensures that individuals can receive the necessary care and services to enhance their quality of life, allowing them to focus on spending precious moments with their loved ones.

In conclusion, Medicare's coverage for hospice care is a vital resource for retirees and their families facing end-of-life situations. It offers comprehensive services and support tailored to meet the needs of the patient, ensuring a dignified and comfortable experience during their final days. Understanding these benefits can provide peace of mind and assurance to retirees and their families as they navigate this difficult journey.

Hospice Care Services and Eligibility Criteria

When facing a serious illness, it is crucial to have access to quality end-of-life care that focuses on comfort and support. Hospice care provides comprehensive services for individuals with a life expectancy of six months or less. In this subchapter, we will discuss the benefits of hospice care services and the eligibility criteria to help retirees and their families understand how Medicare can assist in this challenging time.

Hospice care aims to enhance the quality of life for patients by addressing their physical, emotional, and spiritual needs. It includes a multidisciplinary team of healthcare professionals, such as doctors, nurses, social workers, counselors, and trained volunteers. These professionals work together to provide pain management, symptom control, emotional support, and guidance to both patients and their families.

To qualify for Medicare coverage of hospice care, individuals must meet specific eligibility criteria. Firstly, the patient must be eligible for Medicare Part A (hospital insurance). They must also receive a certification from their doctor and the hospice medical director, stating that they have a life expectancy of six months or less if the illness runs its normal course.

Hospice care can be provided in various settings, including the patient's home, a hospice facility, a nursing home, or a hospital. Medicare covers all necessary hospice services, including medication for pain relief and symptom management, medical equipment and supplies, skilled nursing care, and counseling or social work services.

It is important to note that while under hospice care, Medicare will not cover curative treatments for the terminal illness. However, Medicare will continue to cover treatments for health issues unrelated to the terminal diagnosis.

Additionally, Medicare provides respite care for caregivers. This allows caregivers to take a break from their caregiving duties, knowing that their loved one is receiving professional care in a Medicare-approved facility for up to five days.

Understanding the benefits of hospice care and its eligibility criteria can provide retirees and their families with peace of mind during a challenging time. By utilizing Medicare coverage for hospice care, individuals can access comprehensive end-of-life services that focus on comfort, support, and dignity.

Chapter 12: Medicare Coverage for Durable Medical Equipment

Understanding Durable Medical Equipment (DME)

As retirees and their families navigate the complex world of Medicare, it is essential to have a thorough understanding of the various benefits and coverage options available. One crucial aspect of Medicare coverage is the provision of Durable Medical Equipment (DME). In this subchapter, we will delve into the details of DME, its significance, and how it can benefit you and your loved ones.

DME refers to equipment and supplies that are prescribed by a healthcare professional to aid in the treatment of a medical condition or illness. These items are intended for long-term use and are essential in maintaining a certain quality of life. Medicare recognizes the importance of DME and provides coverage for a wide range of equipment, including but not limited to wheelchairs, walkers, hospital beds, oxygen equipment, and prosthetic devices.

To qualify for Medicare coverage of DME, you must meet certain criteria. Firstly, you need to be enrolled in Medicare Part B, as DME is typically covered under this component of Medicare. Additionally, the equipment must be deemed medically necessary by a healthcare professional and prescribed for use in your home.

It is important to note that while Medicare covers DME, certain conditions apply. For instance, Medicare will only cover DME from approved suppliers who have met specific quality standards. It is crucial to ensure that you acquire your DME from these approved suppliers to avoid unnecessary expenses and complications.

Furthermore, Medicare generally covers 80% of the approved amount for DME, leaving you responsible for the remaining 20% as well as any deductible or co-payment amounts. To alleviate the financial burden, you may consider supplemental insurance options such as Medigap plans, which can help cover these out-of-pocket expenses.

Understanding the coverage and benefits of DME is essential for retirees and their families. By being aware of the equipment and supplies that Medicare covers, you can make informed decisions about your healthcare needs and ensure that you have access to the necessary tools for managing your medical conditions effectively.

In summary, Durable Medical Equipment (DME) is a vital component of Medicare coverage for retirees. It encompasses a wide range of equipment and supplies necessary for managing medical conditions and improving quality of life. Understanding the criteria for coverage, approved suppliers, and potential out-of-pocket expenses will empower you to make the most of your Medicare benefits and ensure that you receive the DME you need.

Medicare Coverage for DME

As retirees and their families navigate the complexities of Medicare, it is crucial to understand the various aspects of coverage that the program offers. One essential component is Medicare coverage for Durable Medical Equipment (DME), which plays a vital role in maintaining the health and well-being of individuals in need of specialized medical equipment.

DME refers to medical equipment that is used for medical reasons, can withstand repeated use, and is appropriate for use in the home. This includes items like wheelchairs, walkers, hospital beds, oxygen equipment, and more. Medicare provides coverage for DME under certain circumstances, ensuring that beneficiaries can access the equipment they need to manage their health conditions effectively.

To qualify for Medicare coverage for DME, beneficiaries must meet specific requirements. Firstly, the equipment must be deemed medically necessary by a healthcare professional. This means that the equipment is necessary to treat or manage a medical condition and is not primarily for convenience or comfort. Additionally, the DME supplier must be enrolled in Medicare and meet all applicable quality standards.

Under Medicare Part B, which covers medically necessary services and supplies, DME is typically covered at 80% of the Medicare-approved amount. This means that beneficiaries are responsible for the remaining 20% as coinsurance. It is important to note that the 20% coinsurance can be supplemented by supplemental insurance options, such as Medigap policies, to reduce out-of-pocket costs.

However, it is essential to understand that not all DME is covered by Medicare. Certain items, such as grab bars, shower chairs, and stair lifts, are considered convenience items and are not covered. Additionally, Medicare may only cover rental or purchase costs for equipment, depending on the specific item and the length of time it is needed.

To ensure coverage for DME, it is crucial to work with a Medicare-approved supplier who understands the intricacies of the program. These suppliers are knowledgeable about Medicare guidelines and can help beneficiaries navigate the claims process seamlessly.

By understanding Medicare coverage for DME, retirees and their families can make informed decisions about their healthcare needs. Whether it is a wheelchair for mobility or oxygen equipment for respiratory support, Medicare ensures that beneficiaries have access to the necessary DME to maintain their independence and quality of life.

Types of DME Covered by Medicare

Durable Medical Equipment (DME) plays a crucial role in the lives of many retirees, providing them with the necessary tools and devices to maintain their independence and enhance their quality of life. Medicare recognizes the importance of DME and offers coverage for a wide range of equipment that is deemed medically necessary. In this subchapter, we will explore the various types of DME covered by Medicare, ensuring that you have a comprehensive understanding of the benefits available to you.

Medicare covers a diverse array of DME, including but not limited to:

1. Mobility Aids: Medicare provides coverage for wheelchairs, walkers, scooters, and canes to assist individuals with mobility impairments. These aids enable retirees to move around independently and engage in daily activities with ease.

2. Respiratory Equipment: Medicare covers oxygen equipment, ventilators, and nebulizers for individuals with respiratory conditions. These devices help to improve breathing and manage respiratory ailments.

3. Blood Sugar Monitors: Medicare offers coverage for blood glucose monitors and test strips for beneficiaries with diabetes. These devices are essential for monitoring blood sugar levels and managing the disease effectively.

4. Hospital Beds: Medicare covers hospital beds for individuals with specific medical needs. These beds are adjustable, allowing for better comfort and care at home.

5. Prosthetic Devices: Medicare provides coverage for prosthetic limbs, including artificial arms, legs, and eyes, enabling retirees to regain functionality and resume their daily activities.

6. Orthotic Devices: Medicare covers orthotic devices such as braces, splints, and shoe inserts. These aids assist individuals in managing musculoskeletal conditions and improving mobility.

7. Medical Supplies: Medicare covers a range of medical supplies, including wound dressings, catheters, and ostomy bags, ensuring that retirees have access to the necessary materials for self-care.

It is important to note that Medicare has specific guidelines for coverage, including the requirement that the equipment is deemed medically necessary and prescribed by a healthcare professional. Additionally, some equipment may require prior authorization or meet certain criteria for coverage.

Understanding the types of DME covered by Medicare is essential for retirees and their families. By being aware of the available benefits, you can make informed decisions about your healthcare needs and ensure that you have access to the necessary equipment for a comfortable and independent lifestyle.

Chapter 13: Frequently Asked Questions about Medicare

Common Concerns and Questions from Retirees

As retirees and their families navigate the complex world of Medicare, it is common to have concerns and questions about various aspects of the program. In this subchapter, we will address some of the most common concerns and questions that arise from retirees regarding Medicare and its benefits.

One of the primary concerns for retirees is understanding the different parts of Medicare and what they cover. Medicare is divided into several parts, including Part A, which covers hospital stays and skilled nursing facility care, and Part B, which covers doctor visits and outpatient services. Additionally, there are prescription drug coverage options available through Part D, as well as Medicare Advantage plans that provide an alternative way to receive Medicare benefits. We will detail each of these parts in the following chapters to provide a comprehensive understanding of the coverage options available.

Another concern often expressed by retirees is the cost of Medicare and how to navigate the various premiums, deductibles, and co-pays. Understanding the costs associated with Medicare can be confusing, but we will break down each component and provide useful tips on how to save money and make informed decisions about your healthcare coverage.

Many retirees also have questions about Medicare supplemental insurance options, also known as Medigap policies. These policies are designed to fill the gaps in coverage left by Medicare Parts A and B, helping to pay for services such as co-pays, deductibles, and coinsurance.

We will explore the different Medigap plans available and help you determine which one may be best suited to your individual needs.

Additionally, retirees and their families often want to know about Medicare coverage for preventive services, chronic disease management, mental health services, home healthcare, skilled nursing facility care, hospice care, and durable medical equipment. We will provide detailed information about each of these topics, including what services are covered, how to access them, and any limitations or requirements that may apply.

Navigating the world of Medicare can be overwhelming, but with the right information and guidance, you can make informed decisions about your healthcare coverage. In the following chapters, we will delve deeper into each of these concerns and questions, providing you with the knowledge and resources you need to make the most of your Medicare benefits.

Answers and Clarifications about Medicare Benefits

Medicare can be a complex system to navigate, often leaving retirees and their families with numerous questions. This subchapter aims to provide answers and clarifications about various aspects of Medicare benefits, addressing the concerns of retirees and their families.

Medicare: Benefits for American Retirees

Medicare is a federal health insurance program that primarily caters to individuals aged 65 and older. It consists of several parts, including Part A (hospital insurance), Part B (medical insurance), Part C (Medicare Advantage plans), and Part D (prescription drug coverage). This subchapter will delve into each part, explaining their benefits and coverage options.

Medicare Prescription Drug Coverage

Prescription drug coverage, also known as Part D, is essential for retirees who require regular medications. We will discuss the different plans available, how to choose the most suitable one, and how to navigate the "donut hole" coverage gap that some beneficiaries may encounter.

Medicare Advantage Plans for Retirees

Medicare Advantage plans, or Part C, offer an alternative to original Medicare. This subchapter will explore the benefits of Medicare Advantage, including additional coverage options such as dental, vision, and hearing care. We will also discuss eligibility requirements and the process of enrolling in a Medicare Advantage plan.

Medicare Supplemental Insurance Options

Medicare supplemental insurance, also known as Medigap, helps cover the gaps in original Medicare coverage. We will provide an overview of the different Medigap plans available, their benefits, and how to choose the most suitable one based on individual needs and preferences.

Medicare Coverage for Preventive Services

Preventive services play a crucial role in maintaining good health as retirees age. This subchapter will outline the preventive services covered by Medicare, such as vaccinations, screenings, and counseling, and how beneficiaries can take advantage of these services to stay healthy and proactive in their healthcare.

Medicare Coverage for Chronic Disease Management

Managing chronic diseases becomes increasingly important in retirement. We will explore the Medicare coverage options for chronic disease management, including medications, specialized therapies, and ongoing care, offering guidance on accessing and utilizing these resources.

Medicare Coverage for Mental Health Services

Mental health is an essential aspect of overall well-being, and Medicare recognizes this. We will shed light on the mental health services covered by Medicare, such as counseling and therapy, ensuring retirees have access to the support they need.

Medicare Coverage for Home Healthcare Services, Skilled Nursing Facility Care, and Hospice Care

This subchapter will delve into the coverage options available for home healthcare services, skilled nursing facility care, and hospice care under Medicare. We will explain the qualifying conditions, coverage limitations, and the process of accessing these services, providing peace of mind to retirees and their families.

Medicare Coverage for Durable Medical Equipment

Durable medical equipment, such as wheelchairs, walkers, and oxygen tanks, can greatly enhance the quality of life for retirees. Here, we will discuss Medicare coverage for durable medical equipment, including eligibility criteria, coverage limits, and the process of obtaining these essential items.

In this subchapter, we aim to address the diverse concerns of retirees and their families regarding Medicare benefits. By providing clear answers and clarifications, we hope to empower our readers to make informed decisions and maximize the benefits they are entitled to under this vital program.

Chapter 14: Resources and Assistance for Medicare

Government Resources for Medicare Information

As a retiree or a family member of a retiree, navigating the complex world of Medicare can be overwhelming. With so many different options and coverage areas to consider, it's crucial to have access to reliable and accurate information. Thankfully, the government provides a wealth of resources to help you make informed decisions about your Medicare benefits. This subchapter aims to guide you through the various government resources available for Medicare information.

1. Medicare.gov: The official website for Medicare is a valuable resource for retirees and their families. It offers comprehensive information on Medicare coverage options, enrollment periods, and how to find healthcare providers in your area. The website also provides tools and resources to compare different plans and estimate your out-of-pocket costs.

2. Medicare & You Handbook: This handbook is sent to all Medicare beneficiaries each year. It contains detailed information about Medicare coverage, including the different parts of Medicare, eligibility requirements, and how to navigate the enrollment process. It also includes a directory of Medicare-approved providers.

3. State Health Insurance Assistance Programs (SHIPs): SHIPs are state-based programs that offer free counseling and assistance to Medicare beneficiaries. Trained counselors can provide personalized guidance on Medicare options, help with claims and billing issues, and explain how Medicare works with other insurance coverage you may have.

4. Social Security Administration: While not solely dedicated to Medicare, the Social Security Administration plays a crucial role in administering the program. Their website provides information on eligibility, enrollment, and how to apply for Medicare benefits. You can also visit your local Social Security office for in-person assistance.

5. Medicare Publications: The Centers for Medicare & Medicaid Services (CMS) produces a wide range of publications that provide detailed information on specific Medicare topics. These publications cover everything from prescription drug coverage to home healthcare services. You can find these publications on the CMS website or request printed copies by mail.

By utilizing these government resources, retirees and their families can gain a better understanding of their Medicare benefits. Whether you're looking for information on prescription drug coverage, mental health services, or durable medical equipment, these resources will help you make informed decisions about your healthcare needs. Remember, knowledge is power when it comes to navigating the Medicare system, and these government resources are here to support you every step of the way.

Non-profit Organizations and Advocacy Groups

In this subchapter, we will explore the invaluable role of non-profit organizations and advocacy groups in supporting retirees and their families. These organizations play a crucial role in educating, empowering, and advocating for the rights and well-being of retirees, ensuring access to quality healthcare and other essential services. Let's delve into some of the key areas where non-profit organizations and advocacy groups make a significant impact.

One of the primary focuses of these organizations is advocating for Medicare benefits for American retirees. They work tirelessly to ensure that retirees are aware of their rights and entitlements under Medicare and assist them in navigating the complex healthcare system. These groups provide valuable resources, such as educational materials, workshops, and one-on-one counseling, to help retirees and their families make informed decisions about their healthcare coverage.

Furthermore, non-profit organizations and advocacy groups also specialize in specific niches within the realm of Medicare. For instance, they provide comprehensive information on Medicare prescription drug coverage, explaining the nuances of different plans and helping retirees choose the most suitable option for their medication needs. They also assist in understanding Medicare Advantage plans, which offer additional benefits beyond the traditional Medicare program.

Medicare supplemental insurance options are another area where these organizations offer guidance. They explain the various supplemental plans available and help retirees select the one that best complements their Medicare coverage.

In addition to coverage options, non-profit organizations and advocacy groups focus on preventive services, chronic disease management, mental health services, home healthcare, skilled nursing facility care, hospice care, and durable medical equipment. They provide detailed information on what is covered under Medicare for each of these services, ensuring that retirees are aware of their rights and can access the care they need.

These organizations also act as a platform for retirees to voice their concerns and advocate for policy changes that benefit them. By mobilizing their collective strength, they influence policymakers to improve Medicare coverage, enhance access to healthcare, and protect the rights of retirees.

In conclusion, non-profit organizations and advocacy groups serve as lifelines for retirees and their families, providing invaluable support, education, and advocacy. Their efforts empower retirees to make informed decisions about their healthcare coverage and ensure that their voices are heard. By working in collaboration with these organizations, retirees can navigate the complexities of Medicare and access the benefits they deserve.

Medicare Counseling and Assistance Programs

As retirees and their families navigate the complexities of Medicare, understanding the available counseling and assistance programs can be invaluable. These programs provide support and guidance to ensure you make informed decisions about your healthcare coverage. In this subchapter, we will explore the various Medicare counseling and assistance programs that are designed to help you maximize your benefits and access the care you need.

One of the key programs available to retirees is the State Health Insurance Assistance Program (SHIP). SHIP offers free, personalized counseling and assistance to Medicare beneficiaries and their families. Trained counselors are available to answer your questions, provide information on Medicare benefits, and help you compare different plans. They can also assist you in understanding your rights and resolving any issues or disputes that may arise.

Another important resource is the Medicare Rights Center, a nonprofit organization that provides free information and counseling to Medicare beneficiaries. Their counselors can guide you through the complexities of Medicare, help you understand your coverage options, and assist with any billing or claims issues you may encounter. They also offer educational materials and online tools to help you make informed decisions about your healthcare.

In addition to these national programs, many states have their own counseling and assistance programs tailored to local needs. These programs offer personalized guidance on Medicare benefits, enrollment, and coverage options specific to your state. They can help you navigate the complexities of Medicare in your area and ensure you access the resources and services available to you.

It is important to note that Medicare counseling and assistance programs are not affiliated with any insurance company or plan. They provide unbiased information and support to help you make decisions that best suit your individual needs and circumstances.

By taking advantage of these counseling and assistance programs, retirees and their families can gain a deeper understanding of their Medicare benefits and make well-informed choices. The guidance and support provided by these programs can help you navigate the complex world of Medicare with confidence, ensuring you receive the care and coverage you deserve.

In the following subchapters, we will delve deeper into specific aspects of Medicare, such as prescription drug coverage, Medicare Advantage plans, supplemental insurance options, coverage for preventive services, chronic disease management, mental health services, home healthcare, skilled nursing facility care, hospice care, and durable medical equipment. Stay tuned to further expand your knowledge on these important topics and make the most of your Medicare benefits.

Chapter 15: Tips and Strategies for Maximizing Medicare Benefits

Understanding Medicare Plan Options

Medicare is a comprehensive healthcare program designed to provide coverage for American retirees and their families. With various plan options available, it is essential to have a clear understanding of Medicare to make informed decisions about your healthcare needs. In this subchapter, we will delve into the different Medicare plan options and their benefits.

Medicare offers several coverage options to meet the diverse healthcare needs of retirees. These options include Medicare Prescription Drug Coverage, Medicare Advantage Plans, and Medicare Supplemental Insurance.

Medicare Prescription Drug Coverage, also known as Medicare Part D, provides coverage for prescription medications. It is crucial for retirees to understand the formulary and cost-sharing requirements of their specific plan to ensure optimal coverage at affordable costs.

Medicare Advantage Plans, or Medicare Part C, provide an alternative to Original Medicare. These plans often include prescription drug coverage and additional benefits like dental, vision, and hearing services. Retirees considering Medicare Advantage plans should carefully evaluate the network of providers and the specific benefits offered by each plan.

Medicare Supplemental Insurance, also known as Medigap, helps cover the gaps in Original Medicare coverage. These plans help pay for out-of-pocket costs such as deductibles, copayments, and coinsurance. Understanding the different Medigap plan options and their standardized benefits is crucial for retirees seeking additional coverage.

Additionally, this subchapter will explore Medicare coverage for preventive services, chronic disease management, mental health services, home healthcare services, skilled nursing facility care, hospice care, and durable medical equipment. Medicare provides coverage for a wide range of preventive services, including screenings, vaccinations, and annual wellness visits, to help retirees stay healthy and catch potential health issues early on.

For retirees managing chronic conditions, Medicare offers various programs and services to support their needs. Medicare coverage for mental health services is also available, ensuring access to counseling, therapy, and mental health screenings.

Moreover, Medicare covers home healthcare services for those who require medical care or assistance at home. This includes skilled nursing care, physical therapy, and occupational therapy. Similarly, Medicare offers coverage for skilled nursing facility care for individuals who need short-term rehabilitation or long-term care.

In the final sections of this subchapter, we will explore Medicare coverage for hospice care, which provides comfort and support for terminally ill patients, and coverage for durable medical equipment, such as wheelchairs, walkers, and oxygen equipment.

Understanding the various Medicare plan options and their associated benefits is crucial for retirees and their families. By having a comprehensive understanding of Medicare coverage, retirees can make informed decisions that best suit their specific healthcare needs, ensuring peace of mind and access to quality healthcare services throughout their retirement years.

Tips for Choosing the Right Medicare Plan

Choosing the right Medicare plan can be a daunting task for retirees and their families. With so many options and coverage variations available, it is crucial to make an informed decision that best suits your healthcare needs. Here are some tips to help you navigate through the process and find the Medicare plan that fits you perfectly.

1. Assess Your Healthcare Needs: Start by evaluating your current health condition and anticipate any potential changes in the near future. Consider your prescription drug usage, chronic conditions, and any specific healthcare services you might require. This will help you determine the type of coverage you need.

2. Understand the Different Parts of Medicare: Medicare consists of several parts, including Part A (hospital insurance), Part B (medical insurance), Part C (Medicare Advantage plans), and Part D (prescription drug coverage). Familiarize yourself with the coverage and benefits offered by each part to identify which ones are most relevant to your needs.

3. Research Medicare Advantage Plans: Medicare Advantage plans offer an alternative to Original Medicare by providing additional benefits and coverage options. Explore the various Medicare Advantage plans available in your area and compare their costs, networks, and additional benefits to determine if they align with your needs.

4. Consider Supplemental Insurance Options: Medicare supplemental insurance, also known as Medigap, can help fill the gaps in coverage left by Original Medicare. Research the different Medigap plans and compare their costs, coverage, and benefits. This can provide you with added financial security and peace of mind.

5. Review Coverage for Preventive Services: Medicare offers several preventive services, such as screenings, vaccinations, and wellness exams, at no additional cost. Ensure that the Medicare plan you choose covers these services to promote proactive healthcare management and early detection of potential health issues.

6. Evaluate Coverage for Chronic Disease Management: If you have a chronic condition, such as diabetes or heart disease, ensure that your Medicare plan covers the necessary medications, treatments, and specialized care required to manage your condition effectively.

7. Assess Mental Health Coverage: Mental health is an essential aspect of overall well-being. Make sure your chosen Medicare plan includes coverage for mental health services, such as counseling or therapy, to address any psychological or emotional needs.

8. Consider Home Healthcare and Skilled Nursing Facility Coverage: If you prefer receiving medical care at home or anticipate needing skilled nursing facility care in the future, verify that your Medicare plan covers these services. Understanding the limitations and requirements of coverage is crucial.

9. Explore Hospice Care and Durable Medical Equipment Coverage: For end-of-life care, ensure that your Medicare plan includes coverage for hospice care. Additionally, check if your plan covers durable medical equipment, such as wheelchairs or oxygen tanks, to assist with your day-to-day needs.

By following these tips, retirees and their families can make an informed decision when choosing the right Medicare plan. Taking the time to assess their healthcare needs, understand the various coverage options, and research the available plans will help ensure that they select the plan that best meets their requirements. Remember, finding the right Medicare plan is about finding the peace of mind and security to enjoy a healthy retirement.

Strategies for Reducing Medicare Costs

As retirees, managing healthcare expenses can be a major concern. However, there are several strategies you can implement to help reduce your Medicare costs without compromising on the quality of care. In this subchapter, we will explore various approaches you can take to make the most of your Medicare benefits and save money in the process.

1. Regularly review your Medicare plan: Medicare plans change annually, and it's crucial to assess your coverage each year during the open enrollment period. By comparing different plans, you can ensure you have the most cost-effective option that meets your specific needs.

2. Utilize preventive services: Medicare offers coverage for a wide range of preventive services such as vaccinations, screenings, and annual wellness visits. By taking advantage of these services, you can catch potential health issues early on, which could save you money on costly treatments down the line.

3. Consider generic drugs and mail-order options: If you require prescription medication, opting for generic drugs can significantly reduce your out-of-pocket expenses. Additionally, exploring mail-order pharmacy services can often provide cost savings and added convenience.

4. Explore Medicare Advantage plans: Medicare Advantage plans can offer comprehensive coverage, including prescription drugs and additional benefits like dental and vision care. By comparing different Medicare Advantage plans, you may find one that better suits your needs while potentially lowering your overall healthcare costs.

5. Evaluate Medicare supplemental insurance options: Medicare supplemental insurance, also known as Medigap, can help cover the gaps in your original Medicare coverage. These plans can help reduce out-of-pocket costs, such as deductibles and coinsurance.

6. Make use of home healthcare services: In certain situations, receiving healthcare services at home can be a more cost-effective option compared to hospital stays or skilled nursing facilities. Medicare covers a range of home healthcare services, including skilled nursing care, therapy, and medical equipment.

7. Utilize community resources and support: Many communities offer programs and resources that can help reduce healthcare costs for retirees. These may include senior centers, clinics, and organizations that provide discounted or low-cost services.

By implementing these strategies, you can effectively manage and reduce your Medicare costs while still receiving the care you need. Remember to stay informed about any changes in your coverage and explore all available options to make the most of your Medicare benefits as a retiree.

Chapter 16: Conclusion

Recap of Medicare Benefits for American Retirees

As retirees, navigating the complexities of Medicare can often feel overwhelming. With numerous options and coverage details to consider, it can be challenging to understand what benefits are available to you and how they can support your healthcare needs. In this subchapter, we will provide a comprehensive recap of Medicare benefits for American retirees, ensuring you have a clear understanding of the coverage options available to you and your family.

Medicare: Benefits for American Retirees

Medicare is a federal health insurance program that primarily serves individuals aged 65 and older. It provides coverage for various healthcare services, including hospital stays, doctor visits, prescription drugs, and preventive care. Understanding the different parts of Medicare, including Part A (hospital insurance), Part B (medical insurance), Part C (Medicare Advantage plans), and Part D (prescription drug coverage), is essential in maximizing your benefits.

Medicare Prescription Drug Coverage

Medicare Part D offers prescription drug coverage to help retirees afford necessary medications. This coverage is provided through private insurance companies approved by Medicare and can significantly reduce out-of-pocket costs for prescriptions.

Medicare Advantage Plans for Retirees

Medicare Advantage plans (Part C) are an alternative to Original Medicare (Part A and Part B). These plans are offered by private insurance companies and provide all the benefits of Original Medicare, as well as additional coverage options such as vision, dental, and hearing services. Medicare Advantage plans often have lower out-of-pocket costs and may include prescription drug coverage.

Medicare Supplemental Insurance Options

Medicare Supplement Insurance, also known as Medigap, is designed to fill the gaps in coverage left by Original Medicare. Medigap plans help cover expenses such as deductibles, copayments, and coinsurance, providing retirees with greater financial security.

Medicare Coverage for Preventive Services

Medicare provides coverage for a range of preventive services, including screenings, vaccinations, and annual wellness visits. These services are crucial in detecting and preventing potential health issues before they become more serious.

Medicare Coverage for Chronic Disease Management

For retirees managing chronic conditions such as diabetes or heart disease, Medicare offers coverage for ongoing care and management. This includes doctor visits, medications, and specialized treatments to help individuals maintain their health and well-being.

Medicare Coverage for Mental Health Services

Mental health is an essential aspect of overall well-being, and Medicare recognizes this by providing coverage for mental health services. This includes counseling, therapy, and inpatient services when necessary.

Medicare Coverage for Home Healthcare Services

Retirees who prefer to receive healthcare services in the comfort of their own homes can benefit from Medicare's coverage for home healthcare.

This includes skilled nursing care, physical therapy, and assistance with daily activities.

Medicare Coverage for Skilled Nursing Facility Care

Medicare provides coverage for short-term stays in skilled nursing facilities after a hospitalization. This coverage ensures retirees receive the necessary care and rehabilitation services before transitioning back to their homes.

Medicare Coverage for Hospice Care

For individuals with terminal illnesses, Medicare offers coverage for hospice care. This compassionate care provides support and comfort to both the patient and their family during the end-of-life stage.

Medicare Coverage for Durable Medical Equipment

Retirees who require durable medical equipment, such as wheelchairs, walkers, or oxygen supplies, can benefit from Medicare's coverage. This ensures access to necessary equipment and reduces the financial burden associated with purchasing or renting these items.

Understanding and maximizing your Medicare benefits is crucial for retirees and their families. By comprehending the various coverage options available, such as prescription drug coverage, Medicare Advantage plans, and supplemental insurance, retirees can make informed decisions about their healthcare needs. Furthermore, being aware of Medicare's coverage for preventive services, chronic disease management, mental health services, home healthcare, skilled nursing facility care, hospice care, and durable medical equipment ensures that retirees have access to the necessary care and support throughout their retirement years.

Importance of Regularly Reviewing and Updating Medicare Coverage

As retirees and their families, it is crucial to understand the importance of regularly reviewing and updating your Medicare coverage. Medicare is a complex system that offers a range of benefits, from prescription drug coverage to hospice care, and it is essential to stay informed about any changes or updates that may affect your coverage.

One of the primary reasons for regularly reviewing your Medicare coverage is to ensure you are receiving all the benefits you are entitled to. Medicare plans and coverage options can change from year to year, and it is essential to stay updated on any updates or alterations that may impact your healthcare needs. By reviewing your coverage annually, you can identify any gaps or areas where you may need additional coverage, such as prescription drugs or chronic disease management.

Regularly updating your Medicare coverage can also help you save money. Medicare Advantage plans and supplemental insurance options can vary in cost and coverage, and by reviewing your options, you may be able to find a plan that better suits your needs and budget. Additionally, by reviewing your coverage, you can ensure you are taking advantage of any available discounts or cost-saving programs that may be available to you.

Another crucial reason to review and update your Medicare coverage is to ensure you are receiving the appropriate care for your specific healthcare needs. Medicare coverage for preventive services, chronic disease management, mental health services, home healthcare services, skilled nursing facility care, and hospice care can all play a significant role in your overall well-being. By reviewing your coverage regularly, you can ensure you have the necessary coverage to manage any existing health conditions or receive the care you need for optimal health.

Lastly, keeping your Medicare coverage up to date can provide peace of mind for both you and your family. Knowing that you have comprehensive coverage that meets your healthcare needs can alleviate stress and allow you to focus on enjoying your retirement years.

In conclusion, regularly reviewing and updating your Medicare coverage is of utmost importance for retirees and their families. By staying informed about any changes or updates, you can ensure you are receiving all the benefits you are entitled to, save money, receive appropriate care for your healthcare needs, and have peace of mind knowing you have comprehensive coverage. Take the time to review your coverage annually and make any necessary updates to ensure you are getting the most out of your Medicare benefits.

Final Thoughts and Encouragement for Retirees and Their Families

Congratulations! You have reached an important milestone in your life - retirement. It is a time to relax, enjoy the fruits of your labor, and spend quality time with your loved ones. As you embark on this new chapter, it is crucial to ensure that your healthcare needs are adequately met. In this final section, we would like to leave you with some key thoughts and encouragement regarding Medicare and its benefits for American retirees.

Medicare is a comprehensive healthcare program designed specifically for individuals aged 65 and older. It provides a range of benefits, including prescription drug coverage, Medicare Advantage plans, supplemental insurance options, and coverage for preventive services. These services are crucial for maintaining your overall health and well-being during your retirement years.

One of the essential aspects of Medicare is its coverage for chronic disease management. As we age, the likelihood of developing chronic conditions increases. However, with the right healthcare support, you can effectively manage these conditions and enhance your quality of life. Medicare offers coverage for various chronic disease management programs, ensuring that you receive the care and support you need.

Additionally, Medicare recognizes the importance of mental health services. Retirement can bring about significant life changes and emotional challenges. Medicare provides coverage for mental health services, including therapy and counseling, ensuring that you can seek the help you may need during this transitional period.

Furthermore, Medicare coverage extends to home healthcare services and skilled nursing facility care. These services are designed to provide you with the support and care you require in the comfort of your own home or in a specialized facility. Whether you need assistance with daily activities or require more intensive medical care, Medicare has you covered.

Lastly, Medicare coverage includes hospice care and durable medical equipment. These services are focused on maintaining your comfort and dignity during end-of-life care. Hospice care offers support for both you and your family during this challenging time, while durable medical equipment ensures that you have access to the necessary aids and equipment to enhance your daily living.

In conclusion, as you enter retirement, it is crucial to understand and utilize the various Medicare benefits available to you. From prescription drug coverage to chronic disease management, mental health services to home healthcare, and hospice care to durable medical equipment, Medicare has comprehensive coverage for all your healthcare needs. Embrace this new chapter in your life with confidence, knowing that Medicare will be there to support you every step of the way. Enjoy your retirement and make the most of this well-deserved time with your loved ones!